LOCAL SCHOOLS OF THOUGHT

LOCAL SCHOOLS OF THOUGHT:
A SEARCH FOR
PURPOSE IN RURAL EDUCATION

by

Clark D. Webb
Larry K. Shumway
R. Wayne Shute

Clearinghouse on Rural Education and Small Schools
Charleston, West Virginia

Clearinghouse on Rural Education and Small Schools
Appalachia Educational Laboratory
PO Box 1348, Charleston, WV 25325

ISBN 1-880785-14-5

Illustrations by John MacDonald, Williamstown, MA
Cover design by Richard Hendel, Chapel Hill, NC

Library of Congress Cataloging-in-Publication Data

Webb, Clark D.
Local schools of thought : a search for purpose in rural education /
by Clark D. Webb, Larry K. Shumway, R. Wayne Shute.
    p. cm.
Includes bibliographical references.
ISBN 1-880785-14-5
    1. Education, Rural—United States.   2. Education—United States—Aims and objectives.   3. Teachers—United States.   4. Educational leadership—
United States.   I. Shumway, Larry K., 1954-   II. Shute, R. Wayne.   III. Title.
LC5146.5.W43   1996
371'.01'0973—dc20
95-45043
        CIP

This book contains a fictional account of an individual teacher's experiences. It is entirely the product of the authors' imaginations; any resemblance to real people, places, or events is entirely coincidental.

This publication was prepared with funding from the U.S. Department of Education, Office of Educational Research and Improvement, under contract no. RR93002012. The opinions expressed herein do not necessarily reflect the positions or policies of the Office of Educational Research and Improvement or the Department of Education.

The ERIC Clearinghouse on Rural Education and Small Schools is operated by the Appalachia Educational Laboratory (AEL), Inc. AEL is an affirmative action/equal opportunity employer.

Interviewer: What would be your approach to improving education?

Wendell Berry: I'd change the standard. I would make the standard that of community health rather than the career of the student. . . . [Now] we're teaching as if the purpose of knowledge is to help people have careers or to make them better employees, and that's a great and tragic mistake. . . . Adding to knowledge is not the first necessity. The first necessity is to teach the young . . . the knowledge that people have in their bones by which they do good work and live good lives (Fisher-Smith, 1994, p. 12-13).

Table of Contents

Foreword

The title of this book—*Local Schools of Thought*—pays homage to Rexford Brown's 1991 book, *Schools of Thought: How the Politics of Literacy Shape Thinking in the Classroom*, which dealt with similar themes. Webb and colleagues depart from Brown, however, and the difference is worth noting. *Local Schools of Thought* especially honors the local circumstance, and that is why the context of the discussion and the persons of the drama live in a rural place and work in a small school.

A couple of warnings are in order. First, this is not a neutral work; it represents the authors' commitments and it speaks in their own well-considered voices. The institutional disclaimer most certainly applies. Second, this volume is not the final word on anything; it is part of a larger conversation about what education is and, ultimately (in Wendell Berry's words,) "what people are for." Such issues are sometimes seen as too abstruse or too remote from education in rural and small schools. And that is one reason we asked for this manuscript.

Clark Webb, Larry Shumway, and Wayne Shute, discuss exactly what they believe to be the purpose of education and the action that teachers and administrators need to undertake to realize that purpose. The purpose is simple. Education should cultivate meaning. Meaning requires of students and teachers the disposition "to go beyond what is known." The idea of "going beyond" is enjoying something of a renaissance these days. The concept has a lot to do with imagination, insight, and empathy. These qualities, surely, are needed more than ever in order to enable the good work that needs to be done in the world.

Local Schools of Thought, in particular, illustrates the good and difficult work that teachers can do when provoked to go beyond the merely evident. That is the secret that the authors disclose and explain as Coach Don Terry, within these pages, confronts challenges familiar to most teachers and administrators.

Craig Howley, Director
ERIC Clearinghouse on Rural Education and Small Schools

Preface

> In [the class entitled] Achievement in English, the students listen or sleep while the teacher reads aloud, for the entire period, portions of a paperback book on motorcycle gangs (Cohn & Stephano, 1985, p. 312).

The scene detailed by Cohn and Stephano happened to be found in a rural setting; nevertheless, every reader knows that such classrooms can be found in every setting, from huge city to tiny hamlet. We believe this scene captures the most debilitating feature of schooling in America: the acceptance of mindlessness as a classroom regularity. The mere fact that such a scene actually occurred in any school anywhere is cause for outrage. Yet, as Cohn and Stephano report the incident, nothing particularly unnerving was considered to be taking place. How is this possible? What have we come to in our educational thinking that we can not only envision such a despairing reality, but tolerate it—with perhaps a knowing, resigned shrug of the shoulders, intended to signify our disapproval but also our acceptance of *reality*? Our purpose in this volume is to make it difficult for readers to avoid examining themselves in terms of the mindlessness illustrated in this tableau.

Instead of devising a manual on the "Reform of Schools," perhaps with its models, steps, strategic planning guidelines, and implementation plan, we intend to raise questions that provoke mindful attention to fundamental purposes and to the creation of meaning. In so doing, we delineate—and thereby indict—the pervasive attitude that encourages the irresponsible and immoral pedagogy found in the class referred to above. An understanding of the inherent dangers of allowing a model-driven mindset to guide teaching, leading, and learning in schools can move an educator to make a genuine difference in the one person central to the success of America's schools—one's self.

The gulf between these two modes of improving—on the one hand the description of models, programs, and procedures with *guarantees* of success; and, on the other, the thoughtful creation of a palette of ideas for the reader's own mindful consideration—is no minor chasm, either. It constitutes an unbridgeable canyon.[1]

Three ideas underpin our writing and will be explicated in the balance of this book:

- Perspective drives action.
- Meaning—personally constructed—is at the heart of everything done in the schools. It is all-important, not only for students, but for teachers, school leaders, and patrons.
- The one educator in whom we can actually produce change is one's self.

Our invitation to you is captured whimsically by Robert Frost (1914) in "The Pasture":

> I'm going out to clean the pasture spring;
> I'll only stop to rake the leaves away
> (and wait to watch the water clear, I may):
> I sha'n't be gone long.—You come too.

We ask you to join us as we attempt to "clean the pasture spring" called American public schools. We have no way of knowing how you will respond as you read this little work, of course. We would feel fulfilled if you were to consider the book as we now do: A journey toward clarity of thought about significant educational matters.

---

[1]Interested readers are referred to the following works (see Works Cited): Brown, *Schools of Thought,* Postman, *Technopoly*; Smith, *Insult to Intelligence*; Solway, *Education Lost.*

CHAPTER 1

A Framework for Considering Local Education

W est Plains is located 140 miles south of the state
capital at an important highway nexus created by
Interstate 64 and U.S. Highways 79 and 40. The
community has much of the heritage common to small towns in
the state: Settled by pioneering families in 1866, its streets are
laid out in orderly squares oriented to the four points of the
compass.

West Plains is a hub for the northern part of Adams County.
Redfern and Spring City, smaller communities of fewer than
1,000 residents each, lie respectively six miles to the north and
south. Redfern Elementary School closed in 1970; Spring City
Elementary outlived Redfern by a year. Now the children of all
three communities attend West Plains Elementary, West Plains
Middle School, and North Adams High School. The enrollment
at North Adams High School has fluctuated between 250 and
300 throughout the past 10 years.

In the mountains north of West Plains, Consolidated Fuel
Company operates the East Fork Canyon Mine. The coal, 3
million tons annually, is hauled by truck to a railhead 75 miles
away. When the mine is operating at peak capacity, a coal truck
rolls past Doug's Foodtown on Main Street every 90 seconds,
around the clock.

Coal provides good jobs. A miner can start at an annual salary near $40,000; coal truck drivers earn almost as much. Consolidated Fuel and the trucking companies generally require employees to have high school diplomas; those in management usually hold four-year college degrees. Other than the Consolidated Fuel management and local school teachers, few people in West Plains are college educated.

There have been more prosperous times in West Plains. In 1987, a landslide in East Fork Canyon demolished the railroad tracks connecting the central part of the state to the east-west main rail lines. The Union Pacific Railroad depot now stands abandoned next to several vacant warehouses on the west side of town.

The theater on Main Street, the Pamela, has closed, as have many other small town theaters, a victim of videotape and cable television. To see a first-run movie, residents drive 20 miles to Ridgefield, the county seat, where one can also find discount stores and the national fast-food franchise outlets. Most residents also go to Ridgefield for medical care; West Plains Hospital closed in 1972.

The West Plains Progress *runs 1,200 copies of its weekly edition. Publisher Kendall Ashland came from the eastern part of the state five years earlier to buy the paper and now worries about the future. Looking from the window of his office, Kendall says, "If many more businesses in town close, the newspaper won't be far behind." Most of the paper's revenue comes from local business advertising.*

During the week, at Doug's Foodtown, townspeople stop to visit as they make their meat purchases over the butcher counter. Doug Faerber describes how he started school in the first West Plains school building. "The old school used to stand right here where my store is," he says over the counter. "We tore it down in '68 and built this store in '69. So I haven't lived my whole life on this spot—just 99 percent of it!"

On autumn Friday evenings, the football field lights are on for varsity games at North Adams High School, and on winter nights the gymnasium is full for boys' and girls' basketball. For West Plains, Redfern, and Spring City, the high school (especially high school athletics) provides a center for community pride and social life.

On evenings after games, Main Street is busy with high school kids cruising. They are in twos or threes in pickups with hunting rifles in the rear window gun racks. Many of the boys wear cowboy hats and T-shirts emblazoned with rodeo advertising. The girls they're with wear tight jeans and their boyfriends' letter jackets. Friendly banter passes between vehicles as they move slowly up and down the highway through town. In some of the abandoned lots on Main Street, four or five pickups are parked, with kids congregated nearby listening to country music on their car stereos.

The scene is familiar to one of the high school teachers, George Campbell. George was raised in a small town in neighboring Wallace County. Even with his own rural background, he was surprised by the narrowness of the experience of the young people in West Plains. "One of the things that strikes me, even though I went to a small high school myself," George says, "is how isolated from reality or the rest of the world students here seem." Very few of them have traveled outside of the state. Those who have went only to Disneyland.

Steve Hansen, another faculty member at the high school, is typical of many West Plains residents. He graduated from North Adams High School in 1978 after winning the state high school wrestling championship and returned to teach at the high school in 1986. By his own definition, he's a lifer. "Lifers," says Steve, "are people who were raised in West Plains. So were their parents, and everything associated with the tradition of the town is important to them, and they are very proud of the area. Don't try to change tradition if you want to get along around here!"

In a small school, the same individual may coach several sports, and that is the case at North Adams High, which has a staff of only 17 teachers. Don Terry has coached his boys' basketball teams to state championships two of the last four years, and the football team has not fared badly. Don came to North Adams High from a state to the north in 1984. He was hired the same year as Mrs. Franklin, the principal. He thinks of Mrs. Franklin as his boss and considers her a decent enough administrator. Don's relationship with his colleagues is characterized by friendly conversation over lunch in the faculty room, horseshoe pitching at the occasional staff cookout, and discussions of administrative details in faculty meetings. Thoughtful talk of teaching among faculty is rare. Yet, Don feels his association with his coworkers is closer than one would find in a typical city school. He sees these people frequently outside of school; knows their spouses and children; and, for the most part, respects them as moral, competent, caring people.

On his way home from work, Don often stops at Doug's Foodtown to pick up a few items. Nearly everyone knows "Coach Terry," and Don stops in almost every aisle to talk with the parents of his students and with other townspeople. Some days, the conversation relates to ball games, some days to something else; some days it seems to Don that all people can do is complain about either "those kids in school these days" or the school's limitations.

Scholastically, things are not that bad at the high school. The best kids at North Adams High can compete with students anywhere. Just last year, the student body president received a regents scholarship at the state university. Still, Don finds the kids in his classes remarkable mostly for their lack of ambition or motivation.

Don loves coaching and doesn't mind teaching. When Mrs. Franklin hires new teachers for North Adams High, she always makes sure they are willing and able to sponsor an activity or help coach a sport. With few shoulders to carry it, the load of teaching and sponsoring extracurricular activities is much heavier for each teacher at North Adams High than it might be in a larger school. But, like Don, most of the teachers are dedicated to their work. And, if asked, they would probably say they are generally satisfied with the school.

Our Perspective

No sense can be made of discussions about schools in West Plains or elsewhere that are not grounded in purposes. Why do we have schools? Our answer is that, essentially, schools exist to help young persons discover, and create, their own being. That is, schools are for creating meaning and fostering understanding—understanding of one's self, of one's fellow beings, and of the world. The principal means to that end is the development of mind.[1]

In writing these words, we do not propose an academic elitism, nor do we espouse a view of humanity limited to its cognitive ability. We believe the mind is the *starting point* for personal progress and that its development allows for success in all facets of life—the arts, one's occupation, family life, citizenship, and the community. Our ability to dream and to create are dependent on the work of the mind, on our "acquiring, retaining, and extending knowledge" (King & Brownell, 1966, p. 20).

Central to our understanding of the work of the mind, which we see as the essence of schooling, is the notion of *going beyond*. Hannah Arendt's comment is to the point: "We are what men have always been—thinking beings. By this I mean. . . that men have an inclination, perhaps a need, to think *beyond the limitations of knowledge*, to do more with this ability than to use it as an instrument for knowing and doing" (1978, p. 12, emphasis added).

By asserting the strong claim of the mind on the rural school curriculum, we disavow a popular cry about school purpose; namely, that it is—or ought to be—economically centered. This view, which can be called "economism," constitutes the reigning paradigm of educational purpose. According to Alan DeYoung (1995, p. 356),

> American rural schools have historically been involved with adapting children to the world of work, first as rural populations flocked into regional population centers, and today as they are challenged to create career-oriented rather than place-oriented citizens.

---

[1]Some educators who have written extensively about these matters are Fullan, 1991; Gardner, 1991; King & Brownell, 1966; Perkins, 1992; and Sizer, 1992.

Education for meaning, as Wendell Berry suggests, must respect, rather than repudiate, local circumstances; and it must contribute on a local basis to community, rather than undermine it. Economism in education makes it difficult, if not impossible, to sustain meaningful and thoughtful instruction.

Examples of the ideology of economism at work abound. James W. Guthrie, Dean of the Graduate School of Education at the University of California at Berkeley, spoke at a recent international conference on educational leadership. One sentence from his remarks captures his uncompromisingly economic perspective on schooling: "Regardless of the variety of national tactics, the western world objective is the same. The long-run goal for policymakers is to utilize educated intellect as a strategic means for a nation to gain or retain an economically competitive position in the global marketplace" (1990, p. 5).

The lure of the economic perspective is irresistible to many planners. The creators of the Utah Strategic Plan for Education offered the following as one of the four objectives for the state's public school system: "Utah will achieve the highest per household income in America" (State of Utah, 1992, p. 14).

While schooling may have many legitimate ends, including economic development and occupational training, we believe that the prime claim of the curriculum on schools should be the work of the mind. The successful construction of meaning and of understanding on the part of students (and adults in the school, too, for that matter) is the work that constitutes the real purpose for schooling. If schools are made into vocational training centers or, conversely, if they are designed as enclaves for an elite academicism, they can only constrain—not promote—human growth. Healthy people are not exclusively philosophers or employees; they are thoughtful in their everyday lives and *therefore* are honorable and valuable workers.

We hold that schools can be more than places for the "mindstuffing" that some people associate with academic rigor, or the "general track" that is sometimes associated (in reality as well as in mind) with vocational training. While it is neither reasonable nor possible to hold school people accountable for the development of the whole child, they can be held accountable for the creation of an environment that engenders in young people a mindful and thoughtful approach to the world around them.

The Framework

Chapters 2 through 7 comprise our responses to six questions:

1. *What is the significance of perspective or frame of reference for schools?* In Chapter 2 we assert that nothing is more significant than the perspective, or mindset, one brings to teaching and learning. Further, we maintain that it is within our power to examine and to change our perspectives or metaphors.

2. *What is teaching and learning for thoughtfulness?* In Chapter 3 we contrast an approach to public education in which the aim is the acquisition of factual knowledge with an approach we call "thoughtful," in which the aim is to create meaning by *going beyond* knowledge acquired.

3. *What do we expect to see in students whose disposition toward thoughtfulness has been increased as the result of schooling?* Chapter 4 postulates that students who engage in thoughtful teaching and learning will acquire a disposition to be mindful; that is, to weigh evidence, to make connections among ideas, to understand perspective, to find alternatives, and to judge value.

4. *What kind of teacher is needed to bring about thoughtful teaching and learning?* In Chapter 5 we aver that thoughtful learning results from thoughtful settings—settings that begin with teachers who are themselves thoughtful.

5. *What characterizes leadership in thoughtful schools?* The thesis of Chapter 6 is parallel to that of Chapter 5, i.e., that thoughtful teaching results from thoughtful settings—settings that begin with leaders who are themselves thoughtful.

6. *What does our analysis of good rural schools imply about the likelihood of change?* Chapter 7 describes our optimism about the prospects for individual change leading to organizational progress. We express our belief that attempts to change organizations significantly through any other means are doomed.

CHAPTER 2

The Significance of Perspective

*G**raduation at North Adams High School is traditionally held on the Thursday evening before Memorial Day. In the last weeks of school, the rush is on for seniors to finish classes and to complete graduation requirements. North Adams graduates must have completed three years of English and social studies; two years of math and science; and miscellaneous art, physical education, computer literacy, and elective credits equalling 24 Carnegie units.*

For the school's most diligent students, these final days of high school are consumed by intense efforts to prepare for Advanced Placement examinations and to finish research papers for Honors English. It is traditional for the seniors to "pull an all-nighter" in the school library with their Honors English teacher, Ms. Reynolds, during the last week before finals as a ritual show of determination and academic effort. They order pizza and break for videos at midnight; the next day in class, a great display is made of exhaustion from the ordeal.

For other seniors, these last weeks are a desperate struggle to compress into one or two months the work they were expected to have done over the four years of their careers at North Adams High. Some are in the final stages of fulfilling graduation requirements by taking correspondence courses offered by the state university, while others have made arrangements with teachers to make up work in courses previously failed. April and May are months of negotiation, of frantic calls from parents, and of frenzied effort by the school staff.

Coach Don Terry teaches most of the social studies offerings required for graduation from North Adams High School. He is confronted each spring with students pleading for mercy—one of the realities that makes classroom teaching so frustrating for Don. As a football and basketball coach, he is consistently able to get the best from his players, but in his classroom he faces students who just won't do the work, let alone their best. He doesn't ask that much of them, he thinks, and has always passed students who showed the least glimmer of effort. Sixty percent is enough for a "D" if students would just turn in their assignments. Don prepares his classes for the final tests by reviewing with them the very questions that he will ask. Still, his prediction that the class average will be just under 70 percent is usually "right on."

Each year, the pressure is on Don. The students, their parents, and even the school counselor all tell him the same thing—that his is the only class holding a group of students back from graduation. Each year, Don gives these students a stack of worksheets to complete, a list of chapter questions to answer, and a pile of maps to label. Each year, students wade through the makeup work, turning it in just hours before graduation, leaving Don with a stack of papers he probably won't correct, a hollow feeling about his integrity, and, even though the kids will graduate, a sense of having failed.

At graduation, Don sits with the other faculty members on the front row of the sweltering school auditorium and wonders what North Adams High School has taught these kids. Those students graduating at the top of their class sit at the front of the stage, their high achievement signified by the special Honors bandelo around their shoulders. The achievement, Don thinks, may really signify that they understood "the game." They remembered what they needed long enough to do well on tests; they wrote papers as assigned by teachers; and they cared enough about grades to do whatever trivial assignment they might have been given, regardless of how it made them feel. They nearly always did as they were asked.

The middle mass of students, the "average kids," Don has to conclude, just got by. After all, as he has said so often, no student who makes at least the effort to turn in assignments will fail his class. These students really didn't understand much, but they did pass. After four years at North Adams High School, they remain essentially ignorant of the world and unaware of their own potential.

Ultimately, Don realizes, the students sitting there on the stage are those who learned mostly that education and schooling mean doing senseless work because—well, because it is asked for, and you have do what is asked or you don't graduate. Too many, Don concludes, have learned that a high school education, while perhaps useful for getting an entry-level job, is mostly a series of fragmented exercises disconnected from their real lives.

For years, the graduation ceremony has been unsettling for Don, and he finds this year's more depressing than ever. He senses strongly that something is wrong with his teaching and with his school, and he is troubled about it. Yet he can't quite put his finger on what it is.

The Might of Metaphor

David Solway (1993) argues that every time teachers enter their classrooms, their pedagogy is driven by metaphor; that is, a worldview or perspective of what teaching and learning are about. These metaphors are powerful and inevitably drive pedagogical actions. And yet, though they merit examination, research reveals that these powerful perspectives are generally taken for granted (Argyris & Schon, 1974; Smith, 1986, p. 22-25). Professional practitioners, teachers and school leaders among them, are rarely encouraged to raise fundamental questions about their educational perspective.

A familiar example of the power of perspective comes from the life of Helen Keller (1954/1903), as cited by Pribram (1985):

I knew then that w-a-t-e-r meant that wonderful cool something that was flowing over my hand. That living word awakened my soul, gave it light, hope, joy, set it free! There were barriers still, it is true, but barriers that could in time be swept away. I left the well-house eager to learn. Everything had a name, and each name gave birth to a new thought. As we returned to the house, every object which I touched seemed to quiver with life. That was because I saw everything with a strange new sight that had come to me (p. 701-702).

Pribram notes that at the moment Helen Keller was able to name objects, "propositions [could be] formed; remembrances, repentances, and sorrows could be entertained. Subject could be responsible for object, cause could lead to effect" (Pribram, 1985, p. 702). In fact, with the advent of language in her life, Helen began to *see* the world differently. She would thereafter be driven by a radically different conception of the setting in which she found herself.

Pribram notes that it is through language that we are able to form propositions (i.e., concepts) about both ourselves and the world around us, which then allow us to create our perspective on the world. As we interpret the world through experience, we construct a personal view of, or perspective on, the world. Our perspective is both persuasive in shaping our thoughts and powerful in its influence on our actions.

Research on action theory shows that educators everywhere lead and teach according to their theories of action—perspectives, as we have called them. In a striking and critically significant conclusion, Argyris and Schon maintain that "theories of professional practice. . . determine all deliberate behavior" (1974, p. 4). Teachers and leaders who have not carefully examined their own "theories of practice" give up control of their actions to unexamined perspectives. They do not fully understand the implications and deepest meanings of their practices. As Ortega y Gasset warned, "We do not know what is happening to us, and that is precisely the thing that is happening to us—the fact of not knowing what is happening to us" (1958, p. 119).

For example, the teacher who asks his student "Would you like me to refer to you as Negro or as black?" is exemplifying an unexamined—by him—frame of reference. (In the actual event, the student responded intelligently, "I think I would like you to refer to me as Joanne." See Purkey & Novak, 1984, p. 16.)

Educators, of all people, ought to examine the perspectives that drive them as they approach their students. Yet, in spite of the significance of frame of reference in educational life, no evidence suggests that substantial numbers of teachers or leaders understand—or even give much attention to—the perspectives underlying their professional practice. They typically come out of schools of education without having given thoughtful consideration to their perspectives or to the assumptions underlying them. Thus, they generally adopt the standard frame of reference *du jour*.

The Dominant Frame of Reference

These days, the dominant educational frame of reference might best be described as teaching or leading as "method" or "strategy." There is an assumption that the key to effectiveness rests not with the leaders or teachers themselves, but with the various strategies they use to transmit information to achieve their goals. This perspective seems firmly in place throughout society.

The mindset represented by the "strategized" approach to human endeavors such as leading and teaching we call *technocratic*; that is, rule by technique or technology. By so naming the mindset, we are not retreating from the intelligent use of technology, but rather are rejecting the uncritical acceptance of a *pattern of thinking* that proclaims that problems inherent in education or other essentially human enterprises can be solved in the same manner as problems encountered in the building of Buicks.

The features of the technocratic worldview are well known.[3] For example, its basic defining element is technique; that is, "any complex of standardized means for attaining a predeter-

---

[3] Some provocative, educationally relevant writing on the idea of technocracy is found in the works of Barrett (1978), Postman (1992), Saul (1992), Smith (1990), and Solway (1989).

mined result" (Merton, in Ellul, 1964, p. vi). As a consequence, the perspective praises efficiency, productivity, specialization and expertness, specifiability of ends, behavioral outcomes, and measurability (Berger, Berger, & Kellner, 1973), as well as the immediate availability of undifferentiated information (Postman, 1992). Its core assumption is that all human problems, not just certain classes of them, are amenable to efficient solution through the application of systematic, analytic, and programmatic interventions.

The triumph of the technocratic paradigm in education, rural and urban alike, is captured in the statement of a prospective graduate student who recently applied for admission to a degree program in educational leadership at a leading western university. In his letter of application he wrote, "Education, like all human interactions, can be managed using several techniques." Apparently William Barrett had it right: "We may eventually become so enclosed in [the presuppositions of the technical world] that we cannot even imagine any other way of thought but technical thinking" (1978, p. 223).

Armed with only the technocratic perspective, many young educators begin their teaching and leading careers. They search for methods, strategies, aids (audio and visual, low tech, and high tech), and procedures or routines of all kinds in their efforts to impart information or to implement programs contained in the plans of mandated curricula.

The proper assessment of learning is, in this view, based on letter or number grades and, increasingly, on standardized scores: If the children don't do too well, the "problem" can be "fixed" by improving the strategies or tactics being used. Those using this perspective are searching for ways to *indoctrinate* learners (Adler, 1990), not to provoke learning. The potential of influential human relationships is de-emphasized because the technocratic mindset believes that power and influence come from technique.

This technicized mindset is evident in many commercial and public-domain programs. The idea is to give educators ready-made solutions. Too often, these packages make themselves known as solutions looking for a problem.

This mindset is also evident in the words of an apparently

dedicated administrator who, when selected as administrator of the year in his state, was asked to write a proposal for school change. This administrator set forth a "three-phase program that would be long term in nature and stress permanent change" in which groups "would be commissioned to formulate their own plans" to "encourage creativity, enduring repetition, and effort." The aim of this elaborate program—elimination of litter (UASSP, 1995). Perhaps most disheartening in this account is the reductionism applied to the motivations of teachers: "Good results by teachers will be recognized and rewarded with special reserved parking privileges and/or free lunch passes."

We believe this technocratic perspective is flawed for four reasons. First, it is impossible to force learning upon anyone who chooses not to learn. Technocratic schooling, however, treats the learner as one whose behavior can be shaped through scientific programming. Pribram (1985) notes that the extreme of this form of changing human behavior has as its stated philosophical aim to "mathematize, to develop laws [of human behavior] in the image of the mechanistic physics of Newton" (p. 704). Productive learning, however, is the result of a choice made by the learner, not a reaction to formulated techniques imposed upon students.

The second reason the technocratic perspective is unacceptable is that it fails to recognize that there is more to teaching than simply transmitting information. Genuine learning has to do with making sense of the world, of creating meaning—work that is substantially different from simply receiving information. It is not enough to invoke teaching techniques that fill the "registry" of the mind with information (Mitchell, 1984). Good or productive learning means that students engage in personally transforming information into meaning by considering, by pondering, by judging—by *acting on the information.* Describing the difference between being acquainted with an idea and knowing about an idea, James writes, "But when we know about [something], we do more than merely have it; we seem, as we think over its relations, to subject it to a sort of *treatment* and to *operate* upon it with our thought (1952/1890, p. 144).

We do not consider the learning of facts and information to be useless. No mindful weighing of ideas can occur absent the information with which to create the ideas. Transmitting knowledge is part of teaching. But to think of teaching (or leading) as *ending* with the transmission of facts and information is demeaning to our profession. Genuine learning is pointed toward the making of personal meaning; that is, of making sense of the world around us. The same observation holds true for a school leader wanting to influence her staff to explore a new idea about education.

A third reason to reject technocratic teaching methods rests on their lack of respect for the fundamental dignity of the individual. The methods of technocratic pedagogy are reminiscent of the cover art of a recent text on school management: The dust cover depicts students entering a fortress-like schoolhouse constructed from a mass of gears, sprockets, and other mechanical contrivances and dominated by a large clock tower. From a door in the lower left corner, they enter the school-machine; from an opening on the right they emerge, smiling, diplomas and lunch buckets in hand. Students were reduced to "consumer goods," and their schooling to a series of "value-adding" routines.

It is not acceptable to *process* children (or any other member of the human family). Even when the means to be implemented in production-line schooling are shown to be effective, it is always for the short term, for some immediate, palpable goal— the development of a reflex-like skill, perhaps. In the long run, such processes don't help people become more reasonable, caring, or thoughtful. The question is ultimately moral: We reject technocratic methods in teaching and administration as firmly as, and on the same grounds as, Gandhi (in Easwaren, 1973) rejected violence:

> I do not believe in short-violent-cuts to success. . . however much I may sympathize with and admire worthy motives. I am an uncompromising opponent of violent methods even to serve the noblest of causes. I object to violence because when it appears to do good, the good is only temporary, [but] the evil it does is permanent (p. 43).

Finally, our fourth point is that teachers teach and leaders "teach" who *they* are. A person who is not mindful cannot help another become mindful. Helping others grow is difficult precisely for this reason: The leader must *be* what he or she hopes those led will become. No technique or strategy can replace *being*. Although the power of example has been acknowledged in every culture, technocratic formulae for change do not ask of practitioners *personal* change. Technocratic change methods "guarantee" success and often do not demand any special effort on the part of the user. In fact, phrases such as "easy to use" and "sure-fire" abound in the marketing of technique-based methods.

Our praise of thoughtfulness as the standard for teaching and learning springs from an understanding that its value transcends *usefulness* or *significance* or even, *centrality*. We have learned from Hannah Arendt (1978) the generally untold truth—that *thinking is the means to a moral life.* When we avoid thought, perhaps preferring habit or tradition to direct us, we do not simply fail to achieve worthy aims, we actually invite wickedness (Arendt's word). Thoughtlessness, in other words, is not a neutral condition in which principals, teachers, and students find themselves, but a retrograde state assuring that good works will be neither undertaken or accomplished.

Arendt came to this radically different view through observing the trial in Jerusalem of the Nazi Adolf Eichmann. As she dwelt on the consistent pattern of his mindless obedience, his matter-of-factness in the face of repeated horror, she found that a momentous question imposed itself on her: "Could the activity of thinking as such, the habit of examining whatever happens to come to pass or to attract attention . . . be among the conditions that make men abstain from evil-doing?" (1978, p. 5). Later she answers her question affirmatively: "wickedness may be caused by absence of thought" (p. 13).

Obviously, such a conception of mindfulness transforms a discussion of school purposes. It is no longer a question of which set of facts shall be the preferred one, but of how to increase the likelihood of moral actions on the part of school citizens.

Summary

Educators carry into the school and the classroom a perspective on how to "do" education. This viewpoint is powerful, for it directly influences their professional actions: They do not act according to the directives of some five-step process, but rather according to an internal map constructed by them for negotiating the world in which they find themselves. When, as is likely to be the case, the frame of reference is unknown or subconscious, little reasonable hope can be held that the educative outcomes of their practice will be potential-releasing.

The currently accepted educational perspective is founded on a technocratic view of humankind that defines individuals as functionaries or elements in the social mechanism. (See, for example, Gibboney, 1994.) It posits that there is one best way to frame and resolve all human problems. Since that is the case, the reasoning goes, people can and should be controlled by reasonable experts—pedagogical, political, and occupational—for their own good. No wonder that manipulative methods and mechanical techniques abound. "The twentieth century," says John Ralston Saul, "has seen the final victory of pure reason in power." But, he reminds us, "reason is no more than structure. And structure is most easily controlled by those who feel themselves to be free of the cumbersome weight represented by common sense and humanism. Structure suits best those whose talents lie in manipulation and who have a taste for power in its purer forms" (1992, p. 16).

Another viewpoint is available, although it does not seem well understood in the late twentieth century. This view assumes that *human development* is the most important aim of schooling and fosters the development of thoughtfulness—both in the sense of one's use of mind and in the sense of being considerate of others—as the pathway to that development.

Superintendents, principals, teachers, and other school staff members owe it to themselves to understand the two perspectives. But, of course, understanding is not sufficient. They must choose the one that offers the greatest potential for promoting the goal of human development. Thoughtful exploration of both perspectives increases the likelihood of the right choice being made.

CHAPTER 3

The Search for Meaning

C oach Don Terry often finds himself thinking back to *May's graduation ceremony, wondering what it is about school that makes some students so unwilling to do the simple work the school asks of them. In his classes, Don has tried to make it as easy as he can for them. Every answer to the assignments he gives them is right there in the book. All they have to do is look it up. What is so hard about that?*

Don knows these kids well, and what is most perplexing to him is that all of them are pretty good workers in other places. During the summer, he sees young people working at the auto parts store out by the interstate or at the Hungry Boy Drive-In on Main Street, and when he talks to their bosses, they comment on what hard workers the kids are. Many students who come from farm families routinely work 14-hour days in the hay fields. What is it that makes school work so distasteful to these kids when other work seems to engage them so readily?

In late June, Don tries to visit all the boys in the school to encourage them to come out for the football team. He finds Eric Forrester at Packer's Garage, working late into the evening to repair a farm truck. Don has been planning to start Eric at one of the offensive line positions this fall, but the junior needs to finish a summer correspondence course to meet athletic eligibility requirements, and he hasn't started on it yet.

"I'll get it done," Eric says.

Don can't resist asking Eric the question that has been on his mind all summer: "What is the difference between working late at the garage and working on your correspondence course or your other schoolwork?"

"At work," says Eric, "I have to figure things out. And I know it makes a difference, Coach. When the truck comes in, they don't already know what's wrong with it. Heck, they wouldn't bring it in if they knew the problem! I mean, if I don't figure it out right, if I can't make sense of it, then I won't fix it right, and they're counting on me. They need this hay truck."

"And here at the garage, I always know right away if I got it right. I mean, either it runs or it doesn't. It's like in football, you know. I always know right away if I made the play, and so does everyone else on the team."

"Besides," Eric continues, "at school, I just can't see how I'm ever going to need to know all that stuff they teach in some of those classes. Like in history, Coach; I know you tell us the past teaches us lessons about what's happening today, but we never talk about today. We just go on and on about a lot of old stuff. We never solve any problems, like I do here at work. At school, it's just teachers telling me the stuff they want me to put down on the test. We don't ever do anything that matters. You know what I mean, don't you, Coach?"

Don's noncommittal answer belies the fact that ,deep inside, he knows exactly what Eric means.

Meaning

At the heart of what we propose for schools is the *joint construction of meaning by adults and children in the school.* What else would define reasonably a thoughtful small school? The term *thoughtfulness* could point to nothing else, really. If one's learning is nothing more than "a basket of facts"

(Anderson, 1984, p. 5)—that is, incoherent fragments of ideas or conceptions—what chance has one to develop one's potential through the construction of meaning?

We acknowledge that our question proceeds from a perspective on school purpose that is not held by everyone: That individual development in the context of the community is of primary importance. Other purposes yield other questions. For example, the technocratic frame of reference—the currently reigning one—does not ask that we worry about fragmented knowledge, but raises questions of this kind: "Which techniques of instruction are most efficient?" Or, "Will certain instructional practices raise achievement scores?" Most initiatives to "improve" schools clearly evidence this efficiency-productivity frame of reference. The strategic planning models commonly used in the creation of school improvement programs almost guarantee such technocratic leanings. (See Utah State Office of the Legislative Fiscal Analyst, 1992.)

Given our perspective, the situation is intolerable when, in thousands of classrooms—rural and urban alike—teacher-generated questions, short answers, worksheets, and memory-oriented tests predominate (Brown, 1991; Kennedy, 1991; Lanier & Sedlak, 1989). In our feverish rush to cram information into minds, with little regard for either pattern or coherence, we do a great disservice to the individual and, thus, to the community, for the latter can never be anything other than the aggregate of citizens who comprise it.

Although we may not do it with intention or even foreknowledge, when we teach exclusively for information, we teach that it is possible to get something for nothing. We play *Let's Pretend* in the classroom (remember the old Saturday morning radio show?): "Let's pretend you are challenged by this trivial notion from the textbook." "Let's pretend that the teacher is helping us to grow mentally." "Let's pretend that our teachers and students are jointly engaged in 'mind-building,' that they are judging, weighing, meditating on, and considering ideas." Thus might teachers, students, and principals talk about teaching and learning in countless schools across the nation—if they were candid.

The problem is the divorce of the mind from day-to-day life.

As countless commentators in this century—from John Dewey to Rexford Brown—have pointed out, school too often is a place not for meaningful learning but for random social activities, for being with one's friends, or at worst, for the enforced examination of triviality. Some professional educators may be put off by Richard Mitchell's comment in *The Gift of Fire*, but it may be closer to the mark than many of us would like to think:

> Looming behind all of the silly things that we do in schools, and pass off as an 'education,' there is nothing less than a great, pervading spirit of dullness and tedium, of irksome but necessary labors directed completely toward the consolidation of the mundane through the accumulation of the trivial (1987, p. 26).

One of the authors had Mitchell's point brought home to him when his seventh-grade daughter asked him to help her with some history homework. He cheerfully agreed, but as they worked their way through the day's assignment, which consisted of seven worksheets, the incoherent nature of the effort became more and more evident. The work required his daughter to match columns of dates, terms, and events; supply one-word answers; and fill in the blanks—short, simple-minded, unrelated mental operations. After some 45 minutes of this cheerless task, he asked, "Amanda, what did you learn about history from this homework?" The daughter looked at her father smilingly and responded, without a trace of irony, "Oh, Dad, I didn't *learn* anything. It's just schoolwork!"

Too many observers of American schools have come away with judgments corroborating Amanda's artless confession. "School learning is severed from learning and living outside of school," write Lanier and Sedlak (1989, p. 119). The complaint was made frequently by John Dewey, who wrote, "Information severed from thoughtful action is dead, a mind-crushing load" (1916, p. 153). More recently, in a series of powerful indictments (1986, 1988, 1990), Frank Smith has pointed out the inanity of "disconnected" schooling. Here, for example, is his statement on reading instruction:

> Theories were developed to support and justify the new fragmented approach to education. "Subskills" theories were proposed that argued that anyone who wanted to read and write

should master a lot of subskills, which in themselves might be meaningless but which when put together would somehow result in proficiency (1986, p. 91).

The technocratic mentality supporting such theories is prevalent, if not endemic, in the public school curriculum.

The Meaning of Meaning

Before suggesting how both adult and young learners in rural schools may break with the technological mindset to construct meaning jointly, it is necessary to define the broad (and, therefore, potentially slippery) term *meaning*. We define meaning as *coherent significance. Coherent* refers to the quality of holding together, of forming a unified whole, of parts fitting well. *Significance* implies a weight of implication and of importance beyond mere chance. Thoughtful schooling is simply formal education that refuses to encourage learning without personal meaning.

We humans generally expect that some intention larger than the self can be discerned in our day-to-day living. In school or out, we believe that a purpose that gives continuity to our being can be found or created. In Marris' (1986) words, meaning is a complex mental structure that "relates purposes to expectations so as to organize actions—whether the actions are taken or only thought about" (p. vii).

This sense of the term is similar to Viktor Frankl's. In *Man's Search for Meaning,* a volume derived from Frankl's experiences in the horrifying conditions of a World War II Nazi concentration camp, he maintains that meaning is the central reality of human life. Existence itself, not just a balanced life, is predicated on an assumed meaningfulness: With a deprecating glance at behavioristic thinking, Frankl notes, "Man's search for meaning is the primary motivation in his life and not a 'secondary rationalization' of instinctual drives" (1963, p. 121).

Based on the dearth of writing about meaning by educational researchers and journalists, it is apparently considered to be of limited importance, perhaps viewed as a "philosophical" notion or a theory unlikely to bear fruit in the "real" work of the classroom. Yet, in our everyday lives, meaning is so pervasive that it escapes our focus. That is, we take it for granted that our lives revolve around a meaning center, so that for one to say meaning is "really significant" is an invitation to sarcastic comments about one's mastery of the obvious. But someone must consider the obvious, because too much school effort has refused to. Perhaps, "it is with [meaning] as with the air which we breathe: Its very pervasiveness allows us to take it for granted. . . ." (Webb, Shute, & Grant, 1994, p. 5).

"Meaning makes sense of action [by] providing reasons for it" (Marris, 1986, p. vii). Since leaders, teachers, and students take action all day, every day, in schools, no more pertinent question could be asked than how, exactly, meaning is fostered among adults and children in schools. Yet, each of us knows, from personal experience as well as from anecdotal stories and formal research on schools, that those involved, particularly the students, do not say, uniformly, "This all makes sense to me; I can give reasons for these actions" (Howley, 1994).

When we as authors assert that we do not consider ourselves either school- or teacher-bashers, some readers may be suspicious, given our argument so far. The truth is that working in or with the public schools is not only our livelihood but our passion. We know that there are many hard-working, committed teachers and administrators who are blessing the lives of students immeasurably by provoking personal growth through the work of the mind. On the other hand, our own experiences in schools and our reading of a substantial body of literature lead us to believe much work remains to be done.

So, we continue our examination of schooling with a question: If our observation about the absence of meaning as a defining characteristic of schooling is justified, what, exactly, is it that schools are providing in place of personal meaning? We take the inability or unwillingness of many educators to foster meaningful teaching and learning to be evidence that our society is in the grip of another frame of reference—that of technocracy.

Production-line teaching and leading are constituted of precisely the values that we have held to be incompatible with meaningful schooling. Graham's (1988) admonition is to the point:

> Learning is the essence of academic achievement, and it is the universal accomplishment we seek for our young. The achievement will come at different rates and in various forms, but our task is to make sure that it occurs, for it is liberating for the individual both intellectually and personally, and necessary for the society politically and economically (p. 165).

Summary

We hold that the purpose of schooling is the creation of meaning. While meaning cannot be created without knowledge, knowledge—possession of the facts—does not guarantee meaning. By meaning, we refer to *coherent significance*, the development of deep understanding that leads one to see the connections between each fact and the whole. What, then, guarantees meaning? We answer *going beyond information, weighing evidence, judging value, finding alternatives,* and *discovering perspective.*[4] When meaningful teaching and learning are replaced by technocratic practices, it leads to the trivialization of learning and, hence, to boredom and frustration.

Meaning is the glue that can hold schools and communities together. The power of meaning extends beyond schools to encompass the very heart of living. Meaning binds families together, connects generations, brings citizens into communities, and unites the communities of nations.

---

[4] The idea of meaning-making as "going beyond what is given" is explicit in the works of Arendt (1978), Berthoff (1990), Brown (1991), Bruner (1986), Dewey (1966/1916), James (1952), and Mitchell (1984)

CHAPTER 4

Meaningful Student Outcomes

*D*on Terry lies awake at midnight in the sweltering summer heat, the windows optimistically open to the mo-
tionless night air. The doubts he felt in the spring about
the effect of schooling at North Adams High School haven't been
lessened by the passage of time. "I'm really not any worse than
any of the other teachers," he muses silently, "but I can't ignore
the reality that I'm not teaching anything important. I'm wast-
ing the kids' efforts as well as my own." The only thing that
keeps him from driving to the school district office and resigning
is his love of coaching. "Not to mention the house payment," he
reminds himself with a sigh.

Each August, Don manages to get away for a few days on his
own. This year he heads for the high mountain lakes of a
national park a hundred miles south of West Plains and the
mind-clearing meditation of fishing and solitude. He has come
to rely on this ritual to steel himself for the school year ahead.
Don always packs a few books for the evenings alone at his
campfire, so on top of the grub box filled with sodas, bacon, and
beans is this trip's reading. Don's wife has been trying for
months to get him to read The Road Less Traveled *by Scott Peck*

(1978), so her well-worn copy has been tossed in. Viktor Frankl was the subject of a recent PBS broadcast that intrigued Don, so Man's Search for Meaning, *checked out of the county library in Ridgefield, goes in next. The most recent Tom Clancy novel is packed last.*

During the ten years he's lived in West Plains, Don has come to these mountains enough to know where he can be alone, though getting there takes everything his four-wheel-drive pickup has to give. In the thin, clear, pine-scented air, surrounded by mountain lakes fed by melting snow, Don can almost feel his dread of another year of teaching leave him.

After a dinner of freshly-caught trout cooked over the camp-fire, Don stretches out near the blaze to read in the chill evening air. Within minutes, he is engrossed in Man's Search for Meaning *and Frankl's concentration camp experiences, the sounds of night in the mountains blocked from his mind. After some time, he adds logs to the fire and returns to his reading, unaware of the stars spinning across the crystalline night sky.*

He turns the pages back to reread a passage: "It is a peculiarity of man that he can only live by looking to the future . . . and this is his salvation in the most difficult moments of his existence. . . . I remember a personal experience. Almost in tears from pain (I had terrible sores on my feet from wearing torn shoes), I limped a few kilometers with our long column of men from the camp to our work site. I kept thinking of the endless problems of our miserable life." As Don reads of Frankl's struggles to avoid starvation, to escape from the terrible pain and brutality, he can't help but recall the struggles of some of his own ancestors. He thinks of his great-grandmother, who lost her husband and four of five sons during a single week of the Civil War; and of his own father who, when liberated from a Japanese POW camp, weighed only 85 pounds. How could they have faced and survived these horrors?

Don reads on carefully by the flickering light from the nearby flame: "I became disgusted with the state of affairs which compelled me, daily and hourly, to think of only such trivial things. I forced my thoughts to turn to another subject. Sud-

*denly, I saw myself standing on the platform of a well-lit, warm
and pleasant lecture room. . . . I was giving a lecture on the
psychology of the concentration camp!. . . By this method I
succeeded somehow in rising above the situation, above the
sufferings of the moment, and I observed them as if they were
already of the past."*

*Don flips forward a few pages: "Life ultimately means taking
the responsibility to find the right answers to its problems and to
fulfill the tasks which it constantly sets for each individual.
'Life' does not mean something vague, but something very real
and concrete, just as life's tasks are also very real and concrete.
They form man's destiny, which is different and unique for each
individual."*[5]

*Don's mind seems to become as clear as the sky above him.
"It's all about meaning. My teaching must lead students to make
meaning out of the content of my class and out of the experience
of their lives," Don muses, unaware that he is speaking aloud.
"In my own life, I find my meaning in my family and my church.
And when I coach, the meaning is clear for my players, but in my
classroom, I have only vaguely, if at all, made the connection to
meaningfulness. And it is meaning that shapes students' lives."*

*Questions form in Don's mind about how he might bring the
meaning he and his players find in athletics into his classroom.
A commitment to teach differently—to foster the disposition for
meaning in his students—begins to form in Don's heart as he
crawls into his camp bed.*

What Students Should Become

The most central question about schooling addresses what
students can become as a result of their formal education experiences.

Almost everyone rejects the overt outcomes perpetuated by
schooling that encourages students to commit bits and pieces of
information to relatively short-term memory, just long enough

---

[5] Frankl, V. (1963), p. 120-122.

to "show mastery of the material" by repeating what they've been told. Yet, for many, this remains the outcome for most of schooling. The humor in the statement that the difference between "A" and "F" students is that "A" students forget five minutes after the test and "F" students forget five minutes before the test comes from the familiarity of the situation to each of us.

Because such rote schooling outcomes are so widely disdained, many teachers and schools have disguised the preponderance of memorization in schoolwork with such cleverness that both they and their students accept the resulting tasks as real intellectual work. The result is the kind of *Let's Pretend* classroom noted in Chapter 3. The reality is that most schools teach not for student performances of understanding but simply for demonstrations of recall. Consider Howard Gardner's (1991) report of years of educational research: "Even students who have been well trained and who exhibit all the overt signs of success—faithful attendance at good schools, high grades and high test scores, accolades from their teachers—typically do not display an adequate *understanding* of the materials and concepts with which they have been working" (p. 3, emphasis added).

The U.S. Department of Labor Secretary's Commission on Achieving Necessary Skills (SCANS) (1992) issued a series of reports about the skills workers will need to succeed in the workplaces of today and tomorrow. SCANS lists as desirable key student outcomes the ability to (1) frame and solve problems, (2) work in groups, (3) interpret data and correct the operations of complex systems based on those data, and (4) evaluate the quality of one's own work.

Although these aims are worthy of the attention of school people, they are cast within an economically centered schooling paradigm, the premise of which is that schools exist to produce workers. It makes schools an extension of a production system in which children enter as raw material to be processed through an educational factory, managed with statistical quality controls and technological standards, and exit the system ready to be plugged in as workers.

But schools are not "producers"; nor are students "products" to be consumed by any social, economic, or political system.

The economic model of schooling, in which one asks who the *customers* of schools are, thinks of students as value-added objects and applies industrial models of statistical quality control, is foreign to any conception of thoughtful schooling. Such a model dehumanizes students and teachers and ultimately is destructive of its own aims of productivity and efficiency.

A few words about terminology are required. The answers to questions about the purpose of schooling are shaped by the words we choose for the query. Purposes are often discussed in terms of *curricular outcomes* or school system *exit behaviors*, phrases that are burdened with the idea of students as objects to be acted upon. We declare that *schooling is ultimately concerned with helping individuals toward the release of their own unique human potential.* While other institutions, such as family and religious organizations, have primary responsibility in social and spiritual domains, schools have been charged to do their work in the domain of intellect (though the lines are obviously blurred in the scheme of things today). The principal work of schools is to promote the development of the human potential for thoughtfulness (Brown, 1991; King & Brownell, 1966). What other result could hold greater promise for a society?

We must each awaken to our individual thoughtfulness. It is the prerequisite to fulfillment of our human intellectual potential. Maya Angelou (1969), in the autobiographical *I Know Why the Caged Bird Sings,* eloquently describes her own intellectual awakening while recognizing that the schooling experiences of her childhood were essentially separate from it:

> Without willing it, I had gone from being ignorant of being ignorant to being aware of being aware. And the worst part of my awareness was that I didn't know what I was aware of. I knew very little, but I was certain that the things I had yet to learn wouldn't be taught to me at George Washington High School (p. 230).

Students begin to exhibit thoughtfulness in their acceptance of their own ignorance and in a burgeoning awareness of perspective. There is no way to sense one's own limitations if the learning that is drilled into one only exercises the memory. In spite of the vast literature decrying the ineffectiveness of schools, the truth is that schools *are* effective—often with numbing results. The procedural lessons of the classrooms, the lessons embodied in our pedagogical *means,* are no doubt learned and learned well. The upshot is that students value Right Answers and slick routinized solutions to fictional problems devised by others. They do not value the mindful consideration of alternate paths to questions and answers, nor do they learn tolerance for ambiguous solutions. As Wiggins (1989) puts it, "The sign of a poor education, in short, is not ignorance. It is rationalization, the thoughtless habit of believing that one's unexamined, superficial, or parochial opinions and feelings *are* the truth" (p. 57).

The learning that develops when thoughtfulness is honored is less a matter of verbal acquisition and more a matter of self-development. We hope for students who (1) further their superficial knowledge through careful questioning; (2) turn those questions into warranted, systematic knowledge; and (3) develop in themselves high standards of craftsmanship in their work irrespective of how much or how little they "know" (Wiggins, 1989, p. 57).

Students can't possibly know everything. The idea of comprehensiveness in curricula, when taken to an extreme, absurdly places every idea on an equal level of importance. Given the pace at which human knowledge of the world is expanding, learning to act in the face of not knowing is surely at least as important as knowing. Costa believes that we demonstrate "intelligent behavior" when we are prepared to act even when "confronted with questions and problems for which we don't know the answer" (1991, p. 19).

That ideas such as these can be put into practice is shown by one high school faculty in their envisioning of how their students will face their ignorance when they graduate:

> [Our] students will leave this school confident that they have developed the "habits of mind" necessary to meet the challenges of the world into which they enter. These "habits" translate into a series of questions that should be applied to all learning experiences:

1. How do we know what we know? What is the evidence? Is it credible?

2. What is the viewpoint we are hearing, seeing, reading? Who is the author and where is he or she standing? What are his or her intentions?

3. How are things connected to each other? How does this fit in? Where have we heard or seen this before?

4. What if? Supposing that it were different? Can we imagine alternatives?

5. What difference does it make? Who cares? Why should I care? (Central Park East, 1993, p. 1)

A school focused on the development of intellectual habits of thoughtfulness does not preclude students' acquisition of information as part of their learning; in fact, it *requires* it. It does, however, by necessity *reprioritize* such initial information: What is wanted is the going beyond what is given, the considering or thinking *about* that knowledge. Content then becomes the "stuff" with which students construct personal meaning by *imagining* something beyond the world that is presented to their senses. This is a self-awareness, a thinking about thinking, that requires judgment, the very quality that is not fostered in "coverage" or "programmatic" teaching and learning.

If this discussion of teaching for understanding and meaning sounds offensively obvious, perhaps not worthy of your sustained attention, consider that the opposite condition—teaching and learning *without* attention to understanding—has become the *norm* in U.S. schools. It is not an excusable, short-term aberration.

Seeing the work of schools as the development of thoughtfulness and accompanying habits of mind broadens the avenues for schooling success. Traditional content outcome goals and measures have restricted the criteria applied to scholastic achievement. Eisner (1991) argued against narrowly defined views of educational outcomes:

> School programs that create a very narrow eye of a needle through which all children must pass diminish educational equity. Thus the social—and indeed the moral—conditions that ought to

prevail in our schools are those that broaden the eye of the needle and make it possible for all children to discover their aptitudes (p. 17).

Establishing the development of thoughtfulness as the primary goal of schooling also recognizes the constructivist view that ultimately students must make their own judgments about meaningfulness in the world. Bruner (1986) writes, "'World making' is . . . in the end the transaction of meaning by human beings, human beings armed with reason and buttressed by the faith that sense can be made and remade. That makes human culture" (p. 159).

Finally, we ought to direct schooling toward habits of thoughtfulness because our identity, our *self*, is the result of our answers to certain questions—questions framed by us about how we interpret the world, about what has *meaning* for us. In other words, these are questions about a *moral* universe. We are, in Taylor's words, "only selves insofar as we move in a certain space of questions, as we seek and find an orientation to the good" (1989, p. 35). A public school education that promotes behavioral training at the expense of the development of the mind cannot give guidance in raising and answering consequential questions.

What this means for schools is typically overlooked in curriculum guides and papers about school leadership. Significant human learning (that is, learning that *we,* the learners, deem significant) is *directional*—it contributes to our ability to demarcate where we are, "relative to the good" (Taylor, 1989, p. 47). We come from some moral space, we are now in another, and we foresee a future one emerging from the past and the present. Thus, incoherent teaching and learning—the pedagogy of technique—contradicts a fundamental human effort, the development of self.

Another way to consider the situation is to note that mindstuffing or technocratically induced learning has no story line; it is not directional. Such teaching and learning is clearly unwise because, as Taylor writes, "we grasp our lives in a *narrative*" (p. 47, author's emphasis). He continues, "In order to have a sense of who we are, we have to have a notion of how we have become, and of where we are going" (p. 47).[6]

Summary

Schooling outcomes typically are focused on memorized information and are measured by students' abilities to recall on command at test time. These performances do not call for understanding of concepts. Such outcome goals derive from economism and other schooling paradigms that view students as products rather than as people.

Since neither teachers nor students can know everything, schools that focus on content under the pretense of teaching everything of importance to students are guilty of educational fakery. Such outcome goals in schools are destructive to values, to independence, to respect for perspective and diversity, and to individuality.[7]

In place of traditional fact-content priorities as the most important school aims, we propose the priority of making meaning. The conception of schooling that learning should lead to the release of human potential, and particularly to the creation of

---

[6] Recent writing about the power of narrative for teaching and learning is Egan (1989), Polkinghorne (1988), and Smith (1988).

[7] As John Gatto, New York State's teacher of the year in 1990, wrote: I've noticed a fascinating phenomenon in my twenty-five years of teaching—that schools and schooling are increasingly irrelevant to the great enterprises of the planet. No one believes anymore that scientists are trained in science classes, or politicians in civics classes, or poets in English classes. The truth is that schools don't really teach anything except how to obey orders . . . . the institution is psychopathic; it has no conscience. It rings a bell, and the young man in the middle of writing a poem must close his notebook and move to a different cell, where he learns that man and monkeys derived from a common ancestor (1990, p. 24).

meaning, will require that teachers, leaders, and students recognize meaning-making as more important that memorizing disconnected facts and, therefore, change the way they do schooling.

Meaning comes when students go beyond the information that is given by texts or teachers to weigh evidence, judge value, make connections, and understand perspective. Thoughtfulness is displayed in the struggle for understanding, even in the face of not knowing. These are the intellectual dispositions engendered by small schools of thought.

CHAPTER 5

Thoughtful Teachers

E ach year, the school district holds an "Opening Insti- *tute" in the unairconditioned auditorium of the high school in Ridgefield. Coach Don Terry has taught in the Adams County schools long enough to know that the district will bring in an expert from out of state to explain the latest educational magic, or a motivational speaker who will try to convince everyone that, despite what their friends and neighbors are saying, teachers really are good people and teaching truly is the greatest job on the planet.*

Faithful to history, this year's speaker is from California and gives teachers her proven formula for successful classroom management using check marks on the chalkboard. The superintendent follows up by letting everyone know that the district will provide a book by the speaker for each teacher. He says this will assure thorough knowledge and districtwide implementation of this progressive system of student management. In the school van, driving the 20 miles back to West Plains, Don is unusually quiet while the other faculty members joke about the morning's activity. George Campbell, who teaches algebra across the hall from Don, declares, "I'll wait for this book to come out on video!" Ms. Reynolds (no one ever thinks of her by her first name, Annie) defends the speaker with the comment, "I've never had to worry too much about it, but those of you who have these discipline problems might really want to take a closer look at this stuff." Don's fellow coach, Steve Hansen, guffaws at this and says, "Listen to Miss Honors English here! I suggest that we solve these discipline problems once and for all. Let's just take the first kid who's out of line to the cafeteria and have a public electrocution during the first day's lunch. That'll put the fear of God in 'em!"

After lunch, the teachers meet with Mrs. Franklin for the first faculty meeting of the fall. She reminds them that the district is pressuring each school to raise achievement test scores. The tests are to be given in early October, four weeks after the kids return to classes. In future faculty meetings, staff are to create a plan to assure that scores go up this year.

One faculty member suggests taking the week before the test to drill the students on the facts that may be on the test, while another informs his colleagues that he has heard of a "test-taking strategies" unit that is reputed to raise scores by at least 15 percent. Mrs. Franklin passes on suggestions from the district. They propose introducing "the element of competition" by making sure students know how the school's test score aver-age compares to the average of other schools in their athletic league. They have suggested that rewards be given (the middle school, Mrs. Franklin tells them, is giving deserving students days off from school) to students who can increase their scores by at least 10 percent. Someone suggests that local businesses might get together to donate a television or something of like value to be given to the student whose score shows the greatest increase.

Back in his room in the late afternoon, Don thinks about his commitment to teach differently, to coach in the classroom for good intellectual habits rather than to bore kids with junk facts. The day's meetings left him feeling discouraged, not because his colleagues or principal or even his superintendent are not good or caring people, but because not once in the day had there been more than a passing mention of teaching or learning. Somehow, everyone seemed to have forgotten the central purpose for which schools exist. No one even talked about thinking or meaningfulness.

"I'm on my own," Don realizes. For years a sign has hung in his locker room that reads "If it is to be, it's up to me." It means more now to Don Terry than ever before.

Considering Ideas

Becoming thoughtful teachers" is an idea easily enough applauded, but the question of how it is done is not easily answered. A vast commercial enterprise rides the wave of success these days in America by answering our question with ready-mix programs for becoming humane, off-the-shelf programs for "caring" leadership and "proven, practical, easy-to-learn" programs that promise to turn students into thinkers who use the 19 Deep-Thinking Process Skills.

In contrast to this technique-oriented effort,[8] some educators recognize that becoming thoughtful teachers is not a mere matter of method mastery. Rather, it is a matter of habits and propensities being cultivated, of changing one's interior self—quite a different undertaking. In fact, as you have probably concluded by now, thoughtfulness for teachers can be no different from thoughtfulness for *students*. In any individual, it is the interrogative mind in action and the creation of personal meaning.

William Barrett (1978, p. 22), after defining technique as "a standard method that can be taught, . . . a recipe that can be fully conveyed from one person to another," decries our "worship of [that] technique," which leads many to believe that they "have only to find the right method, the definite procedure, and all

---

[8]Though we have settled here for the term *effort*, we explored others such as farce, conspiracy, and evil plot. Frank Smith's *Insult to Intelligence* is a fine exploration of the profit-motivated "effort" carried out by corporations to maintain the primacy of "technique for sale." This "effort" is, in our minds, one of the principal contributions to the de-professionalization of teaching.

problems in life must inevitably yield before it" (p. 24). Or, as Schrag writes, "Learning to be thoughtful is not learning to perform a particular action nor is it acquiring a method of obtaining a particular result; it is developing a 'second nature' which transforms heart and mind" (1988, p. 80). As Don Terry is beginning to see with some clarity, a central element of being thoughtful is making educational purpose central to the work of schooling. To do that, one must actually pay attention to ideas, not just receive and dispense them willy-nilly. Education thus centered is well described by Athanasios Moulakis:

> An education does not consist of turning the candid gaze of the student from one object to another with images of a more or less complex reality registering on a photographic plate. It is rather the active transformation of a mind or more generally, of a sensibility as it seeks to attain a higher degree of discernment and greater coherence within the universe of meaning it inhabits (1994, p. 2).

For some, the notion of educators perceiving the transformation of students' minds as a prime purpose of schooling may be, at the very least, troubling. The nature of the transformation to which we refer is one of nature, not of ideology. It is a change from a state of being unaware to one of being aware—aware of the centrality of meaning to our humanness. And it is, as we have noted above, a transformation that individual *teachers* also must undergo if they are to lead students to thoughtfulness.

Thoughtfulness as a teacher demands continual deepening. Thoughtful teachers recognize that they don't arrive at some final destination of "master teaching." Rather, thoughtful teaching (as thoughtful learning) is a journey in which we continually travel through new, though perhaps familiar, landscapes. There is no "career ladder" for thoughtfulness, but only a process of continuous growth in multiple areas.

Mary Catherine Bateson puts this idea into a provocative passage. About her own writing, she notes:

> Thoughts must be opened into sequential prose. It would not do to lay them out too precisely, however, for I have wanted to convey something of the process of learning, and most learning is not linear. Planning for the classroom, we sometimes present

learning in linear sequences, which may be part of what makes classroom learning onerous: This concept must precede that, must be fully grasped before the next is presented. Learning outside the classroom is not like that. Lessons too complex to grasp in a single occurrence spiral past again and again, small examples gradually revealing greater and greater implications.... Spiral learning moves through complexity with partial understanding, allowing for later returns (1994, p. 30).

Going Beyond What is Given

One of the chief powers of the mind is its ability to pursue thought; that is, to make inferences or draw conclusions from some initial knowledge. William James referred to the mind "operating" on some subject given it (1952/1890, p. 144). One cannot hope for "understanding" simply through having a verbal grasp of a few terms jumbled together. Good educators know this, and they lament the filling of the registry of students' minds through fragmented memorization as contrasted with genuine learning.

Thoughtful teachers provide opportunities for the learner to create meaning; they do not "give" meaning—an impossible task. C. S. Lewis (1947) has argued that if we *were* to find a method by which to give our descendants the unalterable "right" meaning, the end result would be the abolition of man. The imaginative discovery of meaning is the foundation of thoughtful teaching and learning, its defining characteristic. Genuine learning is inevitably a two-stage affair: We receive impressions, names, or descriptions of things and circumstances from the world beyond our minds; we then may go beyond the given, to think about what we have received. This is what Ann Berthoff means when she notes:

Language seen as a means of making meaning has two aspects, ... [naming and telling]. By naming the world, we hold images in mind; we remember; we can return to our experience and reflect on it. In [telling about it,] we can change, we can transform, we can envisage .... We can articulate our thoughts; we can think about thinking and thus interpret our interpretations (1990, p. 21).

This is the great key to mindful teaching and learning: That the learner be encouraged—pedagogically, not just motivationally by exhortation—to go beyond what is given.

Newmann has issued recently a number of reports on thoughtful social studies classrooms (1990a, 1990b, 1991). He determined the "nature of discourse" in nearly 300 social studies lessons in 16 midwestern high schools by having observers note the presence or absence of 15 possible dimensions of classroom thoughtfulness. Newmann's analysis yielded "six main dimensions [of thoughtfulness] . . . as most fundamental":

1. There was sustained examination of a few topics rather than superficial coverage of many.

2. The lesson displayed substantive coherence and continuity.

3. Students were given an appropriate amount of time to think; that is, to prepare responses to questions.

4. The teacher asked challenging questions and/or structured challenging tasks (given the ability level and preparation of the students).

5. The teacher was a model of thoughtfulness.

6. Students offered explanations and reasons for their conclusions (1990b, p. 68-69).

Referring to his overall conceptual scheme for the research, Newmann writes that "the defining feature of higher order thinking" is the "tasks or questions that pose cognitive challenge and require students to go beyond the information given" (1990b, p. 256).

We expect the impossible if we look for students to discover or create meaning without confronting the challenge of considering or interpreting some initial observation. Where baskets of facts are the only harvest from teaching, meaning will not be found. The beginning must be made, of course—the name must be learned, the fact acquired—but learning that dies with the naming (and we do not consider that as wholly figurative language), never has power to develop within young people a sense of mastery—either of world or of self.

A parallel idea is clearly evident in the structure of our language: Until the subject is "completed" by a verb, neither sense nor a sentence is made. Only a primitive form of knowledge of the world (and thus, of knowledge of self) can be communicated. Such sentence fragments are analogous to the learning fragments represented by facts isolated from meaning. In the thoughtful statement of Ann Berthoff, "There is no authentic literacy if it does not serve the making of meaning" (1990, p. 140). Can we feel fulfilled as educators in schools that encourage only "right-answer" givers and discourage maturing, self-confident youngsters who can "give reason" for their thinking?

The sentence—the core of meaningful linguistic expression— is the paradigmatic analogy for meaning-construction, i.e., for thinking that considers, ponders, and weighs. The sentence contains a *something* and a reflection on, or interpretation of, that *something*. So the work of the mind is not only to think, but to also think *about*. Short of that, the mind acts only as a kind of registry, collecting factual bits and pieces, conceptual grunts that are parallel to meaningless sentence fragments.

The grammatical term "predication" that names this completing or asserting action is revealing: It expresses the idea of affirming some basic notion and interpreting it, a "reflexing" of mind. The idea of predication is useful as a criterion by which to distinguish growth-producing teaching and learning. Thus, we want to foster in all potentially educative settings predicative teaching and learning because our uniquely human cognitive ability consists in precisely this—the reflexive consideration of our self in a world. That is the only way we have of making meaning.[9]

"Human behavior above the level of reflex [in our terminology, above the level of naming]," writes Polkinghorne, "is in-

---

[9]Because of the centrality of this concept (predicative teaching and learning), we have included a brief annotated bibliography on the subject (see Appendix).

fected with the features of meaning" (1988, p. 17). For us, therefore, given the supreme importance of such learning, the question for any citizen of a school—youth, teacher, or principal—becomes, "Does the teaching here lead to predicative thinking on the part of students—that is, to thinking that is more than mere word capturing?"

This idea may strike some readers as far-fetched. Some may even believe that it is especially inappropriate for rural teaching and learning, arguing, perhaps, that more direct attention to job-related knowledge is needed. That kind of thinking, we maintain, demeans both teachers and learners. We think those who take exception to the idea of thoughtful (as we have described it) teaching and learning will be persons who, to some degree or other, have fallen into the grasp of the technocratic mindset— thinking of the need to raise scores, to master components of complex skills, to work through programs; persons who believe that meaning is actually yielded by the achievement of learning "objectives."

Of course, we recognize that graduates will be expected to become productively employed individuals who can make their way in the world. But it is precisely the disposition of thoughtfulness that will lead them to be productive. *Change* in the workplace is the one certainty high school graduates can count on. A narrow vocational preparation will yield, at best, persons who can perform specified operations well and solve certain problems. It will not contribute to the mindful flexibility necessary for productivity in the future, which will include new operations and the ability to *frame* problems, not simply solve them. Thoughtless individuals are unproductive, whether as community members, family members, or employees.

Consideration for People

A second element of educational thoughtfulness is being considerate of other people, as when we say that one is a thoughtful associate, meaning that he or she is attentive to the needs of others. This quality Coach Don Terry has believed important for all of his professional life. The following brief vignette (Purkey & Novak, 1984, p. 16) illustrates negatively the idea. In a high school class, the teacher asks a student, "Would you like me to refer to you as Negro or black?" The student responds, "I think I would like to be referred to as Joanne." While the teacher's question could have been innocent, its effect is to set the student apart, to classify her as an instance of a cultural category rather than to see her as a unique, valuable human being.

Joanne's reasonable answer allows all concerned to escape the categorization trap. The point is that, given her apparent classifying mindset, the teacher is unlikely to encourage personal growth in Joanne. The teacher's inability—perhaps unwillingness—to see Joanne as an individual jeopardizes the latter's development as a human being. Such action is at least thoughtless and perhaps more insidious than that.

Teaching is naturally invasive (Gatto, 1992; Howley, 1993); therefore, carried on without respect for learners, it becomes not simply an unproductive, but an anti-social, activity. Lack of respect in the relationship between teachers and students permits a subtle but corrosive power to be exercised in the classroom.

Part of being a thoughtful or considerate teacher is to seek to release the potential of students, to help them realize their dreams. Writing of disadvantaged minority students, Jaime Escalante, the well-known high school math teacher who was the subject of the film *Stand and Deliver*, notes that "a great obstacle [to youth holding to a dream] today is a poverty of faith in the ability of young people to overcome adversity, to achieve, perhaps, what we, as adults, have failed to achieve" (1990, p. 15). Thus, thoughtfulness *toward* students becomes a matter of taking seriously students' intense desires to achieve—*ganas*, in Spanish. Failure to honor their *ganas*, whether of minority or majority students or others, is the kiss of death for . . . .youth and [their advancement]" (p. 15).

Conveying the same idea, Brown writes that a "literacy of thoughtfulness . . . involves both the exercise of thought and a certain amount of caring about other thinkers in past and present communities" (1991, p. xiii). Taking seriously the phrase "other thinkers" would mean treating both adults and students in schools decently and humanely.

Being considerate of students is no new idea. C. S. Lewis (1947) detected the principle in its broadest application in almost all of the world's religions and cultural traditions. In the 1950s and 1960s the idea was described in psychoanalytic terms. For example, "threat-reduction" was advocated to promote "self-growth." To be considerate of students was to allow them to gain self-confidence in their uniqueness. Thus, it was held, significant learning would be fostered. In general, a teacher who is thoughtful toward both adults and students frees or releases energy in those persons so that growth may occur.

An "inviting" school can be envisioned and created in which personal growth is fostered through the mutual consideration shown by people in the school. This is the contention of Purkey and Novak (1984) in *Inviting School Success*. Based on perceptual and self-concept psychology, the ideas of "invitational learning" are offered to help teachers and administrators, as well as students, view each other as able, valuable, and responsible. Such a view is justified because people possess relatively untapped potential in all areas of human development" (p. 2). The potential can be realized by places, policies, and programs . . . designed to invite development, and by people who are personally and professionally inviting to themselves and others" (p. 2).

In connection with another research tradition and focusing on the adults in schools, Little (1990) suggests that when interpersonal consideration is found among the adults in schools (a relatively rare state in her cited studies), the learning environment for students is better organized, the individuals in the workplace are "equipped for steady improvement," and thus "greater coherence and integration of the daily work of teaching" results (p. 188).

Ultimately, consideration of people stands on its own as a prime element of thoughtful teaching. We are not thoughtful towards people so that they will learn more successfully. We are thoughtful of them because it is right. No purpose is required; no justification is demanded. Acting considerately solely as a means to organizational ends devalues every relationship. "A complete relationship needs a covenant . . . a shared commitment to ideas, to issues, to goals," writes Max De Pree. "Covenantal relationships reflect unity and grace and poise. They are expressions of the sacred nature of relationship" (as qtd. in Senge, 1990, p. 145).

Summary

We believe that thoughtfulness is the key to teaching for meaning. At the core of thoughtfulness is a careful attention to language. Language yields meaning and leads to the unfolding of thought. Thoughtfulness is fostered by predicative teaching and learning that always seeks to turn knowledge into coherent meaning by going beyond what is given.

Thoughtfulness, as used here, also refers to the thoughtful consideration of people. Because teaching is a naturally invasive act, respect for students is required of anyone who purports to believe in the dignity of each individual. A school environment inconsiderate of people is unlikely to be considerate of ideas.

Finally, we return to the clearest imperative of all: Teachers must *be* what it is we hope students will *become*. If we hope for thoughtful students to emerge from our schools, these very schools must be inhabited by thoughtful teachers. *To be considerate of both ideas* and *of people*—consider the power of that quality in America's teachers!

CHAPTER 6

Thoughtful Leadership

*E*very morning at 6:00 a.m., Coach Don Terry walks and jogs at the high school track with his wife Karen. They may be alone or a few other couples and individuals may be on the track, depending on the weather. Since coming to West Plains ten years earlier, Don and Karen have been here daily, rain or shine. The time they spend together walking and talking has become so precious that not coming is unthinkable. They discuss their children, finances, plans for the future and retirement, politics, and their latest reading.

On this morning in mid-November, Don is quiet as they jog through the first lap. Karen speaks first.

"You were up later than usual last night," she comments. "Another Tom Clancy novel?"

"No."

After another lap of silence, Karen tries again.

"Have you started a new book?"

"No."

Finally, as they start walking the second mile, Karen asks, "Are you okay, Don?"

"Well, you know I've been doing a lot of reading. And I've been doing a lot of thinking about the motto I've had for my teams all these years: 'If it is to be, it is up to me'."

"Go on," says Karen.

"So I've told you how, in my classes this year, I'm really trying to teach meaningfully for my students. And whenever I've talked to Mrs. Franklin about how we could change a few things to make it easier, I've felt like she didn't even get what I was talking about. Then last night I read some things about problem solving, and I decided that if it is to be, it truly is up to me."

"Karen, I've never given much thought before this year about my teaching, not like I have my coaching. When I think about it, if I coached the same way I've taught in the past, we wouldn't win a game. I mean, I would spend practices teaching kids the weight of the ball, the dimensions of the court, some formula for the trajectory of the ball to the hoop on free throws. We would study the statistics of great games in the past and see films about basketball clubs in Asia. When I coach, my players don't learn stuff like that; they learn to play the game. Even when we do a drill in practice, my players always know exactly where the skill will fit on game day. They learn to create, to go beyond the plays they're given, to understand how things all fit together on the court and in the game. And that's what I have to do in my classes."

"So when I read about solving problems, I saw that it applied to me, and specifically in this situation. I have to recognize what I can control, what I can't control, what I may have to give, and what I may have to give up."

"And you're sure you really want to take this on?" Karen asks.

"I just know I have to if I'm true to myself. And do you know the greatest challenge of it, Karen? I can't fake this. I've never been a great historian, but if I just stayed ahead I was okay. But it's not historical facts that I care about now. It's teaching thinking and building meaning. To do that, I have to think myself. I have to build my own meaning. I can't lead my students somewhere I've never been. And it scares me because I know this new perspective I have will change my work at school."

"So," Karen says, *"it's a little like the old saying that you can lead a horse to water, but you can't make him drink, except in this case you would add that you ought to have drunk from the pond before you try to lead anyone there."*

"You're exactly right on that one," says Don as they finish the
last lap and head for the car.

Leadership Perspectives

Throughout this writing, we have proclaimed the crucial
influence of a thoughtful perspective among citizens of schools.
Its place in thoughtful leadership is no less decisive. Educational leaders who have misconstrued the aim of schooling will,
logically, form a second misapprehension about its leadership.
Thus, a perspective that sees the school as an environment to be
arranged such that students acquire bits of knowledge will also
see the role of educational leadership as a matter of manipulating
organizational and environmental contingencies such that certain "outcomes" are "produced."

Such perspective keeps those who hold it comfortably aloof
from introspection, from thoughtful self-awareness: When the
regnant paradigm prescribes externally devised, even imposed,
rational and technical solutions for all human problems, who is
going to be concerned about the difficult task of coming to grips
with one's integrity? The condition, in turn, makes it more
likely that the nonself-examining leader will seek change by
changing others. Certainly, the passion for molding others in our
image of a better world is strong these days.

As an example of what can result from mindless leadership,
consider a curriculum designed in a real school district in the
grip of thoughtlessness (actually, committee thoughtlessness).
Having decided to implement "character education," leaders
designed a curriculum for "changing others" in which the following objective was typical in content and format:

Objective 8000-0706
Practice personal integrity in all aspects of life and
understand that there is a consequence for every deci-
sion and action.
Date Taught: _____
Date Mastered: _____

When a school leader—the principal, say—accepts this type of approach to learning as worthy pedagogy and offers leadership on behalf of that goal, what will result? Will the principal reason, "I believe that personal integrity is as important as we have represented it to be to students in this curriculum; therefore, it behooves me to make sure that I am honorable in my work with faculty, staff, and students—that I act congruently with my deepest beliefs."? Or will the first thought be, instead, "I've got to make sure that the teachers get the number of integral, sincere, and humane children up to 70 percent because the district office is pushing me on this."?

Unless the development of self is genuinely present and not merely espoused in curriculums, leaders will be unable to resist the lure of the technocratic mindset. Thus, they will convince themselves that good leadership consists of determining some objectives that ostensibly can be measured, mandating the practices that supposedly constitute the means for achieving the objectives, and arranging external conditions of the teaching-learning setting to effect the desired outcome in staff members and students. Having done that, they will be able to tell colleagues (or parents, or lawmakers) that they are "into" school restructuring (or renewal, or values education, or reform).

We offer the following question: Is it possible or conceivable that some "leadership" proffered to improve schools through large-scale change—that is, through renewing, restructuring, or reforming—is in fact a smoke screen to cover an unwillingness to improve a more intransigent setting—namely, oneself?

Leadership of Self

At the heart of thoughtful leadership is the understanding that we can truly control change in only one agent—ourselves. When a leader seeks to create a meaningful school, he first seeks to be certain that he has created meaning in his own leadership and living. When a leader determines to foster thoughtfulness among his teachers, he first determines to foster thoughtfulness within himself.

Thoughtful leadership carries the metaphor of learning

as thoughtful growth. A leader whose own actions and relationships exemplify the personal realization of considerate, careful living creates a palpable reality of the ideas we have been writing about. The hard truth is that unless the leader's professional practice is thoughtful, urging its manifestation in others is not only useless but hypocritical. In other words, the leader must have some personal sense of moral urgency.

We contend that leaders and teachers, who feel a deep sense of "rightness" about schooling for meaning and thinking, will not take this concept lightly. For us, this is no light-hearted foray into educational theory. We view these concepts to be truths, and find the roots of our most pressing social problems in the failure of individuals and institutions to recognize and operate on them.

Our point is that a leader cannot be one kind of person and another kind of principal. Robert Frost expressed this as well as anyone in these lines from *Two Tramps in Mud Time*:

> But yield who will to their separation,
> My object in living is to unite
> My avocation and my vocation
> As my two eyes make one in sight.
> Only where love and need are one,
> And the work is play for mortal stakes,
> Is the deed ever really done
> For Heaven and the future's sake.

Thoughtfulness

Leadership is "rooted in the fundamental enlightenment of thought." So says Richard Gibboney. He goes on to say,

> Learning and teaching, and the seminal ideas and values and exemplary practice that inform them, are all that constitute what is properly the study of education. This is all that any teacher or administrator must know. All else is secondary and supportive. It is these things that enable the managerial eye not only to see but to see with a compelling vision of the future (April 15, 1987).

Of all the things that can and do go on in schools, the work of teaching and learning—what we call the work of the mind—is of greatest importance. The real task for school leaders is to contribute, through their own mindful living, to environments within schools where the work of the mind is the premier undertaking. This means that school leaders first envision, and then help create within their schools, a perspective on teaching and learning in which, in the words of Richard Mitchell (1984), "the mind takes the grasp of itself"; that is, in which there is human potential-releasing learning.

How do school leaders create within their own schools such a metaphor or perspective? We answer by returning to the concept of leadership of self. School leaders create this metaphor in their schools by first creating it within themselves.

Getting one's own leadership life in order, while considerably less glamorous than attempting to restructure an entire enterprise, will, in the long run, be of greater benefit. This is so because of what appears to be a fundamental law of the universe: *You don't get something for nothing.* None of us can lead others to improve unless we ourselves are improving. All the rational programs and all of the technocratic efficiency in the world cannot contravene that law.

Summary

Ultimately, leaders, who would promote thoughtfulness and meaning as a metaphor for schooling, must integrate that metaphor in their own lives. The power of the concepts of unleashing human potential must be made manifest through their own living. A leader who is thoughtful, who manifests meaningfulness in every interaction, is the key to creating schools that manifest thoughtfulness and meaning. One might be a Coach Terry or a Mrs. Franklin. While it is difficult to refute the crucial nature of the leadership from school principals, it is just as difficult to refute the ability of individual teachers to be influential leaders in their school.

Finally, this is a matter of fundamental significance. Thoughtful leadership rests upon the recognition of *truth* in these concepts and a willingness to take up the cause. It is no light thing.

CHAPTER 7

The Outlook for Change

*T*he mail that he gets as a teacher and coach never ceases
to amaze Don Terry. It is usually so irrelevant that he
refuses to look at it, letting it build up in his box in the
office until the school secretary complains that she can't fit any
more in. This evening he has come in after basketball practice
and has mail piled in front of him on the faculty room table.

The blitz of advertisements for an array of products staggers
Don's imagination. In a slick brochure, a textbook company
announces the publication of a new American history volume
aligned with the new national standards and achievement tests.
The publisher assures Don that the use of their curriculum will
make his teaching simple and will result in significant increases
in student achievement. "Great," he mutters. "Won't it be great
to not have to think about what we're teaching?"

Other mail suggests countless ways Don can raise funds for
his programs by selling chocolate, pencils, jackets, discount
coupon books, key chains, and tableware. "Your school can
earn $5,000, $10,000, even $25,000 in just three weeks!" Some-
how, his name is even on a custodial products mailing list, so
lately he has been the target of advertisements for cleaning
solutions, mops, and fluorescent fixtures.

*Then there is the outpouring of bureaucratic mail. The state
attorney general's office informs him of new sexual harassment
complaint procedures for all state agencies, with a special note
to teachers about recent legal proceedings against educators.
The district office asks him to assess the impact of the district's
inservice program on his own teaching. The state high school
activities association provides him with a suggested policy to
prevent fighting among players in athletic contests.*

*Part of the mail seems, at least on the surface, to be related to
teaching and learning—what Don conceives of as the real work
of school. Each day there are several pieces of mail promoting
inservice programs for teachers. One is titled "Increasing
School Achievement: A Failure-Proof Design for School Improvement." Don reads that this workshop would provide him
with* "The Five Elements *that the presenters know to be critical
to the institutionalization of instructional improvement initiatives."*

*Another flyer advertises a series of videotapes (six 20-minute
tapes for $795) titled "Suicide Prevention: Cooperation, Con-
cern, and Communication." The text of the advertisement guarantees that viewing these tapes will provide "administrators,
counselors, teachers, parents, and student leaders with practical, easy-to-use, and proven strategies" for suicide prevention,
as well as "counseling techniques to deal with the difficult
aftermath of suicide situations." He can't help wondering about
"proven prevention strategies" that leave the need for "counseling in the aftermath."*

*Don has come to realize that, unless he finds the right ques-
tions, no "fool-proof" answer is worth a dime. He just hopes he
doesn't drown in the sea of solutions that everyone appears to be
selling!*

*Sitting alone in the school, Coach Terry thinks about his
evolving perspective on schooling. "No one else around me may
see it this way, and perhaps they never will. I may be by myself
in this, but I know what must be done. I can't change anyone
else, but I know for sure that I can change myself."*

The Outlook for Institutional Change

Educational institutions suffer from an addiction to prescriptions. School change for the past five decades has been a nearly perfect record of failure because each effort has depended upon implementing programs or techniques to solve deep-seated philosophical issues at the root of the learning dilemmas in American schools (Gibboney, 1987; 1994).

Barth (1990) described how such prescriptions have not only failed to bring the "cure" to schools, but have actually promoted the further advancement of the disease:

> Our public schools have come to be dominated and driven by a conception of educational improvement that might be called list logic. The assumption of many outside the schools seems to be that if they can create lists of desirable school characteristics, if they can only be clear enough about these directives and regulations, then these things will happen in schools (pp. 37-38).

The chances for real change in the quality of schooling depend on radical changes in our approach to change. Frank Smith (1993) described the difference between problems and disasters: problems bring attempts at solutions, while disasters bring flight. We propose flight from the technocratic methods of educational problem solving and developmental models to a process of personal change founded on the pursuit of individual meaning. This does not mean abandoning all we know; rather, it means acknowledging that all our knowledge, without a deep sense of personal meaning, has little power to change us, thus little power to change schools.

Joseph Conrad in *Heart of Darkness* (1902) creates a picture of futility well-suited as a metaphor for traditional change strategies:

> Once, I remember, we came upon a man-of-war anchored off the coast. There wasn't even a shed there, and she was shelling the bush . . . In the empty immensity of earth, sky, and water, there she was, incomprehensible, firing into a continent. Pop, would go one of the six-inch guns; a small flame would dart and vanish, a little white smoke would disappear, a tiny projectile would give a feeble screech—and nothing happened. Nothing could happen. There was a sense of insanity in the proceeding, a sense

of lugubrious drollery in the sight; and it was not dissipated by somebody on board assuring me earnestly there was a camp of natives—he called them enemies—hidden out of sight somewhere (p. 61).

The Outlook for Personal Change

As authors, we are generally pessimistic about the outlook for widespread institutional change, but optimistic about the outlook for individual change and school-level change. Every educator has experienced this feeling of senselessly wasted energy. Effective change will only come when individual teachers and principals gather the courage to strike out in a direction that separates them from the world of fool-proof methods, easy solutions, and quick cures.

We have deferred to prepackaged notions of education because they are easy. The struggle toward teaching and learning for understanding is hard. But as Scott Peck (1978) wrote,

> Life is difficult. . . . This is a great truth, one of the greatest truths. (The first of the 'Four Noble Truths' which Buddha taught was 'Life is suffering.') It is a great truth because once we truly see this truth, we transcend it. Once we know that life is difficult—once we truly understand and accept it—then life is no longer difficult. Because once it is accepted, the fact that life is difficult no longer matters (p. 15).

The same principle is at work in educational change. Are the ideas in this book and others like it right? Do they make sense to you, or connect to experiences of real learning and understanding in your life? If so, take courage and begin. Draw a line and refuse to go back across it. Accept the challenge of thoughtfulness in all teaching and learning that are in your control. Viktor Frankl (1963), in his description of his experiences in World War II concentration camps, wrote:

> What was really needed was a fundamental change in our attitude toward life. We had to learn, and furthermore, we had to teach despairing men, that it really didn't matter what we expected from life, but rather what life expected from us. We needed to stop asking about the meaning of life and instead think of

ourselves as those who were being questioned by life—daily and hourly (p. 122).

We expect that taking the path toward thoughtfulness, the path that leads to meaningfulness in your school or classroom, will entail a journey of great difficulty. There can be no escape from it, because no great personal growth can come without a corresponding effort and struggle.

The courage needed for this journey includes acceptance of two ideas:

1. Integrity: Change requires honesty in assessing both the learning that has been going on in our classrooms and schools and the teaching we have been doing. So much of schooling is fakery, where teachers have pretended that the "stuff" they were teaching was important, and students and parents, especially those who have gotten "A's" for their submission, have accepted the charade. We must face the reality that we have often been misled.

So much of our sense of professional esteem as teachers comes from our subject matter knowledge. Honesty, however, requires that we see great teaching not as a matter of knowing a lot, but as a matter of artistry, of an ability to lead students in their individual work of making meaning from the flood of fact and feeling in their lives. Honestly exploring what it is to be a great teacher and what real learning is all about is a start.

Since integrity means an undivided whole or the absence of fracture, we cannot claim personal integrity while living one way and professing another. It is not a hypothetical construct but a *truth*—a form of which we learn by living in families—that you cannot provoke allegiance in others to something that you are not willing to demonstrate. Citizens in schools cannot cultivate mindful teaching, learning, and leading in others without themselves *being* mindful.

2. Patience: Our schools have for so long promoted antithoughtful educational practices that many current concepts of "good teaching" are of that ilk. One can hardly fire every nonthoughtful teacher or expel every student who does not yield to understanding. Thoughtfulness cannot be "implemented" or "adopted." It is rather a seed to be planted and nurtured in both ourselves and those around us. As it grows and swells within us, we see its worthiness, which will also become evident to others.

The focus on the individual as the unit of change does not mean that schooling organization is exempt from close examination. Many of the problems in schools today have system origins. Consider Holzman's (1993) observation:

> The school systems themselves are at issue when we think about improving education in this country. These systems are highly complex, surprisingly similar across the country, and very resistant to change. Where once they were the solution to a problem —"inefficiency"—some observers now see them as the problem: antiquated bureaucratic and technical structures that make it difficult to focus on the paradigmatic learning situation, the relationship between the individual teacher and an individual student (p. 18).

It is precisely that relationship—between the teacher and the student—that is dishonored by the technocratic mentality. The following agenda from a school administrative meeting is typical of the sort of systemic failure that seems to have occurred everywhere. (Since this meeting, we have taken to examining agendas from administrative meetings in many other districts, and find them to be astonishingly similar!)

Not one item on the agenda discusses teaching or learning, even though everyone at the meeting would have agreed that these are the most important purposes of schooling organizations. When we begin to think of schooling in terms of a collection of separate problems—management, curriculum, activities, etc.—the meaningfulness of education and the fundamental importance of teacher-learner relationships disappear. In Senge's words,

> From a very early age, we are taught to break apart problems, to fragment the world. This apparently makes complex tasks and subjects more manageable, but we pay a hidden enormous price. We can no longer see the consequences of our actions; we lose our intrinsic sense of connection to a larger whole . . . After a while we give up trying to see the whole altogether (1990, p. 3).

Agenda

Welcome—Superintendent

I. INFORMATION ITEMS

    a. Public Relations—please place this information in your PR Notebooks

    b. U.S. West, Outstanding Teacher Program

    c. Macintosh computer support

    d. Certificate of Outstanding Academic Performance

II. DISCUSSION ITEMS

    a. Earthquake preparedness

    b. Hazardous waste removal and disposal

    c. Hepatitis B and HIV

    d. Equipment needs for next school year due by March 1

    e. UHSAA risk management

    f. Update on masters program

    g. Quality circles request

    h. Staff reduction calendar

    i. Provisional teachers

    j. Status of residential hall

    k. RT/CT follow-up training

    l. Date and time of next meeting

Summary

Changing the way we think about schooling is not something that can wait. The thoughtlessness found in schools affects every aspect of our world. Of course, schools are influenced by society as well as influential in society; they are not the only blameworthy agency contributing to the social malaise that afflicts us. Nevertheless, to the degree they *are* culpable, we should act to counter the unwanted influences present in them.

What we are talking about has an impact not only on pedagogy and the formal organization of schooling. These ideas are powerfully connected to our living in families, to the workings of politics in our society, to the productivity and morality of business, and to the religious or spiritual fabric of our lives. There is a moral urgency to thoughtful schooling that cannot be ignored.

In contrast to the prevalent conception that schools are transformed by changing organizations, our belief is that the critical element is the individual. One at a time, each teacher and principal must make up his or her mind to stand for the full potential of humanity. Educators must determine that they are responsible in their own classrooms or schools to create the setting that will most favor the unleashing of potential in those over whom they have an influence. And having made that determination, they must commit themselves personally to meaning and thoughtfulness.

Afterword

Education is primarily about making meaning, which is not the same as adding to knowledge or even mak[ing] students better employees. Education is about becoming thoughtful toward life so that we, in Wendell Berry's words, "do good work and live good lives." Creating meaning is such a fundamental process that its presence defines our humanity. As Viktor Frankl (1963) and others have maintained, without meaning for the individual, there is no genuine human living.

A Note on the Individual and Community

Much of what we write suggests organizing the learning environment so that the individual can come to understand the enormous power he or she wields through the work of the mind. At the same time, we speak positively about the ideal of *community*. How can we reconcile these apparently discrepant ends? Recognizing the vast scope of the question—how many millions of words treating the topic fill the bookshelves of libraries already?—we modestly propose the following.

Tinder (1980) claims that the ideal of community, although ultimately unattainable, is inescapably part of what it means to be human. In Western society, at least, we seek a goal that is, on the face of it, impracticable: to maintain personal freedom at the same time we experience group unity. Recognizing the dominance of the ideal (in spite of its unattainability), Tinder offers a unique basis on which to build community. "I suggest that we try out a concept unassociated, in many minds, with community: the concept of inquiry" (p. 17). He justifies this unusual suggestion by noting that "man is essentially an inquirer." *Essentially* is the operative word. That is, by virtue of our humanness, we are driven to doubt, to question, to search. Good inquiry is no more than thoughtful searching.

In a twist on the usual assumption about the phenomenon, Tinder insists that inquiry is *not* a solitary practice: Our understanding of inquiry "has been distorted not only by a false intellectualism but also by a false individualism" (p. 17). In fact, he continues, "we are beings in search of being, our own being and that of others"; consequently, we cannot avoid the sense of community in our inquiring efforts.

In the preceding pages, we intended to foster the thoughtful search of personal meaning, but not at the expense of a unified community. With mutual good will and a sensitive respect for (or, at least, civility toward) others, such a goal is possible. For "the desire for individuality and freedom are ultimately the same. This is [the meaning of] interpreting man as an inquirer and community as inquiry" (Tinder, 1980, p. 34).

Although it is true that community can be created in metropolitan settings, we are more likely to think of smaller realities when, for example, Berry speaks of "community health" as the standard for good schooling. He insists that "the teacher, the person of learning, the researcher, the intellectual, the artist, the scientist ... make common cause with a community" (in Fisher-Smith, 1994, p. 13). Although our focus is on rural schools, the kind of effort we urge in this volume is applicable to all teaching and learning situations—K through 12, college, and even less formal educational settings such as the family or church. What powerful idea about teaching and learning is not applicable to every setting? In its simplest formulation, our central message is, "Let's be sensible about—mindful or thoughtful of—what we're about when we do education." So while our ideas are certainly most relevant to small settings, they are ideas for the individual educator in any setting to contemplate. It is precisely the consideration of ideas by individuals that may lead to changed educational practice.

The duality of meaning associated with the word "thoughtful" is revealing about its community orientation: It suggests not only consideration of ideas, but also consideration toward other persons. For example, Rexford Brown found that what leaders most wanted in the people they worked with was "thinkers, people with judgment, people who are thoughtful—about the jobs they are doing, the people they are doing them with, and the people they are doing them for" (1991, p. 1).

The costs are high when we forget that there are mindsets in the world that lead us away from the simple goal of sensible, mindful teaching and learning; mindsets that give an ominous cast to the observation of Ortega y Gasset: "We do not know what is happening to us, and that is precisely the thing that is happening to us—the fact of not knowing what is happening to us" (1958, p. 119).

Appendix

Annotated Bibliography on
Predicative Teaching and Learning

Adler, M. J. (1990). Beyond indoctrination: The quest for genuine learning. In D. D. Dill & Associates, *What teachers need to know: The knowledge, skills, and values essential to good teaching* (pp. 157-165). San Francisco: Jossey-Bass. Indoctrination, rather than teaching, is what takes place typically in classrooms. Learning in classrooms is not always caused by the teacher's activities. Knowledge results from information plus thinking about the information; otherwise only opinion is had. Only teaching that is essentially coaching can result in habits of mind that allow learners to form knowledge.

American Association for the Advancement of Science. (1989). *Science for all Americans: A Project 2061 report on literacy goals in science, mathematics, and technology.* Waldorf, MD: AAAS Books. (ERIC Document Reproduction Service No. ED 309 059, microfiche only)
This is a piece on the pedagogy of science learning. In chapter 13, "Effective Learning and Teaching," the authors lament teachers' willingness to "overestimate the ability of their students to handle abstractions" by assuming that "the students' use of right words [is] evidence of understanding" (p. 146).

Arendt, H. (1978). *The life of the mind.* New York: Harcourt Brace Jovanovich.
Thoughtlessness contributes to evil. For wickedness to occur, nothing more than an unwillingness to consider or judge ideas may suffice: "Wickedness may be caused by absence of thought" (p.13).

"Self-presentation [a matter of conscious thought] would not be possible without a degree of self-awareness—a capability inherent in the reflexive character of mental activities and clearly transcending mere consciousness, which we probably share with the higher animals" (p. 36).
"Judgment," she writes, brings together the general, "always a mental construction," and the particular, "always given to sense experience" (p. 69).
"No mental act, and least of all the act of thinking, is content with its object as it is given to it. It always transcends the sheer givenness of whatever may have aroused its attention and transforms it into . . . an experiment of the self with itself" (pp. 73-74).

Berthoff, A. E. (1990). I. A. Richards and the concept of literacy. In *The sense of learning* (pp. 136-149). Portsmouth, NH: Boynton/Cook.
Philosophy is central to classroom. Teaching and learning are matters of inquiry, of semiotics, and of hermeneutics (interpretation). The signal is not the message in communication theory, nor is the name final learning in schooling: "decoding" is not significant learning. "There is no authentic literacy if it does not serve the making of meaning" (p. 140). "All knowledge is interpretation [and] interpretation is the work of the active mind" (p. 149).

Dewey, J. (1966/1916). *Democracy and education: An introduction to the philosophy of education.* New York: The Free Press.
Chapter 12, "Experience and Thinking," contains a treatment of what we have called herein predicative teaching and learning. For example: "The starting point of any process of thinking is something going on, something which just as it stands is incomplete or unfulfilled. . . . To fill our heads, like a scrapbook, with this and that item as a finished and done-for thing, is not to think. It is to turn ourselves into a piece of registering apparatus" (pp. 146-147).

Gardner, H. (1991). *The unschooled mind: How children think and how schools should teach.* New York: BasicBooks.
Gardner calls for a radical shift in the attention given by

schools to "deep understanding." Maintaining that presently public educators have not shown high interest in fomenting understanding in students, he claims that what we get now in schools are either "natural [or naive] understanding" or "conventional performances." These are to be contrasted with the superior goal of "disciplinary (or genuine) understanding" (p. 9).

Hooke, R. (1987/1665). Preface. *Micrographia*. Lincolnwood, IL: Science Heritage, Ltd.
The great English scientist notes that humans are able both to "behold the works of Nature" *and* to "consider, compare, alter, assist, and improve them." The idea is at the heart of predicative teaching and learning.

Jordan, J. C. (1980). What a sentence is. *Making sense of Grammar*. New York: Teachers College Press.
Clear explanation of what makes a sentence the powerful concept that it is; namely, that it uses both a subject and a predicate. This is the pattern for predicative teaching and learning.

Mitchell, R. (1987). *The gift of fire*. New York: Simon and Schuster.
The "gift of fire" (referring to the Prometheus legend) is our mind's ability to go beyond merely registering sense data; it is our capacity for drawing conclusions, for reasoning, for imagining, and so on. The author calls it "a generally human possibility—the mind's ability to behold and consider itself and its works" (p. 22). He notes later that "it is, rather than a skill, a power and a propensity, both of which can be learned and consciously applied" (p. 36). Mitchell considers education—which is more than schooling—to be "nothing but the nourishment of...moments of thoughtfulness" (p. 22).

Polkinghorne, D. (1988). *Narrative knowing and the human sciences*. Albany: State University of New York Press.
Concerned about the lack of effect on *practical* problem-solving that research in his field, psychology, was having, he went to the practitioners to see what could be learned about research from them. "What I found was that practitioners

work with narrative knowledge" (p. *x*). "Narrative [is] the primary form by which human experience is made meaningful. Narrative meaning is a cognitive process that organizes human experiences into temporally meaningful episodes" (p. 1).

"As an activity the realm of meaning is described by verb forms rather than nouns" (p. 4). That is, "The products of the activity of the realm of meaning are both *names of elements and connections or relations among elements.*"

Polkinghorne intends to show that narrative meaning is a form, perhaps "the" form, of the dual process that we have called predicative learning: "Narrative meaning is created by noting that something is a *part* of some whole and that something is the *cause* of something else" (p. 6).

Pribram, K. (1985). Mind and brain, psychology and neuroscience, the eternal verities. In S. Koch & D. E. Leary (Eds.), *A century of psychology as science.* New York: McGraw-Hill.

This piece contains the statement that what makes us human is "our ability to make propositions, i.e., to conceptualize processes as subjects acting on objects" (p. 702).

Wray, V. (1985). Back to basics: Which one? *National Forum: Phi Kappa Phi Journal, 65*(4), 7-10.

"Good judgment begins with a clarity of vision of the 'things' themselves, the issues, the world." "Good judgment *next* depends upon the ability to form meaningful propositions about clearly named things. . . . Meaning emanates from the marriage of a precisely chosen subject and verb, a union which almost inevitably, of its own power, produces a complement" (pp. 8-9).

Works Cited

Adler, M. J. (1990). Beyond indoctrination: The quest for genuine learning. In D. D. Dill & Associates, *What teachers need to know: The knowledge, skills, and values essential to good teaching* (pp. 157-165). San Francisco: Jossey-Bass.

Anderson, R. C. (1984). Some reflections on the acquisition of knowledge. *Educational Researcher, 13*(9), 5-10.

Angelou, M. (1969). *I know why the caged bird sings.* New York: Random House.

Arendt, H. (1978). *The life of the mind.* New York: Harcourt, Brace, Jovanovich.

Argyris, C., & Schon, D. A. (1974). *Theory in practice: Increasing professional effectiveness.* San Francisco: Jossey-Bass.

Barrett, W. (1978). *The illusion of technique: A search for meaning in a technological society.* Garden City, NY: Anchor Press.

Barth, R. S. (1990). *Improving schools from within: Teachers, parents, and principals can make the difference.* San Francisco: Jossey-Bass.

Barzun, J. (1991). *Begin here: The forgotten conditions of teaching and learning.* Chicago: University of Chicago Press.

Bateson, M. C. (1994). *Peripheral visions: Learning along the way.* New York: Harper Collins.

Berger, P. L., Berger, B., & Kellner, H. (1973). *The homeless mind: Modernization and consciousness.* New York: Random House.

Berry, W. (1986). Does community have value? In R. D. Eller (ed.), *The land and economy of Appalachia. Proceedings from the 1986 Conference on Appalachia.* Lexington: University of Kentucky Appalachia Center. (ERIC Document Reproduction Service No. ED 312 112)

Berthoff, A. (1984). *Reclaiming the imagination: Philosophical perspective for writers & teachers of writing.* Portsmouth, NH: Boynton/Cook.

Berthoff, A. (1990). *The sense of learning.* Portsmouth, NH: Boynton/Cook.

Brown, R. (1991). *Schools of thought: How the politics of literacy shape thinking in the classroom.* San Francisco: Jossey-Bass.

Bruner, J. S. (1986). *Actual minds, possible worlds.* Cambridge, MA: Harvard University Press.

Central Park East Secondary School. (1993). Unpublished papers, Coalition of Essential Schools Fall Forum (November 1993, Louisville, KY).

Cohn, M., & Stephano, A. (1985). Ridgefield High School. In V. Perrone and Associates, *Portraits of high schools: A supplement to high school: A report on secondary education in America.* Lawrenceville, NJ: Princeton University Press.

Conrad, J. (1902). Heart of darkness. *Youth and two other stories.* Edinburgh: William Blackwood and Sons.

Costa, A. L. (1991). *The school as a home for the mind: A collection of articles by Arthur L. Costa.* Palatine, IL: Skylight Publishing.

Dewey, J. (1966/1916). *Democracy and education: An introduction to the philosophy of education.* New York: The Free Press.

DeYoung, A. J. (1995). *Farewell Little Kanawha: The life and death of a rural American school.* New York: Garland Publishers.

Easwaren, E. (1973). *Gandhi, the man.* San Francisco, CA: Glide Publications.

Egan, K. (1989). *Teaching as story-telling: An alternative approach to teaching and curriculum in elementary school.* London: Routledge.

Eisner, E. W. (1991). *The enlightened eye: Qualitative inquiry and the enhancement of educational practice.* New York: Macmillan.

Ellul, J. (1964). *The technological society.* New York: Knopf.

Escalante, J. (1990). Hold to a dream. *Network News and Views: Educational Excellence Network, 9*(2), 14-16.

Fisher-Smith, J. (1994, February). Field observations: An interview with Wendell Berry. *The Sun, 218,* pp. 6-13.

Frankl, V. (1963). *Man's search for meaning: An introduction to Logotherapy.* Boston: Beacon Press.

Frost, R. (1914). The pasture. *North of Boston.* London: David Nutt.

Frost, R. (1936). Two tramps in mud time. *A further range.* New York: Henry Holt.

Fullan, M. (1991). *The new meaning of educational change* (2nd ed.). New York: Teachers College Press.

Gardner, H. (1991). *The unschooled mind: How children think and how schools should teach.* New York: BasicBooks.

Gatto, J. T. (1990, June). Why schools don't educate. *The Sun, 74,* pp. 23-27.

Gatto, J. T. (1992). *Dumbing us down: The hidden curriculum of compulsory schooling.* Philadelphia: New Society.

Gibboney, R. A. (1987, April 15). Commentary: Education of administrators, an American tragedy. *Education Week, 4*(29).

Gibboney, R. A. (1994). *The stone trumpet: A story of practical school reform, 1960-1990.* Albany: State University of New York Press.

Graham, P. (1988). Achievement for at-risk students. In *School success for students at risk: Analysis and recommendations of the Council of Chief State School Officers.* Orlando, FL: Harcourt, Brace, Jovanovich. (ERIC Document Reproduction Service No. ED 305 150)

Guthrie, J. (1990). *Effective educational executives: An essay on the concept of preparation for strategic leadership.* Paper presented at the International Intervisitation Program Conference, 1990, Manchester, England.

Holzman, M. (1993, September). What is systemic change? *Educational Leadership, 51*(1), 18.

Howley, C. (1993). Absent without leave: Solitude and the scheme of schooling. In C. B. Howley, R. W. Shute, & C. Webb, *Thoughtful leadership: Proceedings of the third conference on thoughtful teaching and learning.* Provo, UT: Brigham Young University, Department of Educational Leadership. (ERIC Document Reproduction Service No. ED 374 108)

James, W. (1952/1890). *Principles of psychology.* Chicago: Encyclopedia Britannica.

Keller, H. (1954/1903). *The story of my life.* Garden City, NY: Doubleday.

Kennedy, M. M. (1991). Policy issues in teacher education. *Phi Delta Kappan, 72*(9), 658-665.

King, A. R., & Brownell, J. A. (1966). *The curriculum and the disciplines of knowledge.* New York: John Wiley and Sons.

Lanier, J., & Sedlak, M. (1989). Teacher efficacy and quality schooling. In T. J. Sergiovanni & J. H. Moore (Eds.), *Schooling for tomorrow: Directing reforms to issues that count*, pp. 118-147. Boston, MA: Allyn & Bacon.

Lewis, C. S. (1947). *The abolition of man; or, Reflections on education with special reference to the teaching of English in the upper forms of schools.* New York: Macmillan.

Little, J. (1990). Teachers as colleagues. In A. Lieberman (Ed.) *Schools as collaborative cultures: Creating the future now.* New York: The Falmer Press.

Macrorie, K. (1984). *Twenty teachers.* New York: Oxford University Press.

Marris, P. (1986). *Loss and change, Rev. ed.* London: Routledge & Kegan Paul.

Mitchell, R. (1984). Why good grammar? *National Forum, 65*(4), 4-6.

Mitchell, R. (1987). *The gift of fire.* New York: Simon and Schuster.

Moulakis, A. (1994). *Beyond utility: Liberal education for a technological age.* Columbia: University of Missouri Press.

Newmann, F. M. (1990a). *The relationship of classroom thoughtfulness to students' higher order thinking: Preliminary results in high school social studies.* Madison: Wisconsin Center for Education Research, National Center on Effective Secondary Schools. (ERIC Document Reproduction Service No. ED 326 466)

Newmann, F. (1990b). Qualities of thoughtful social studies classes: An empirical profile. *Journal of Curriculum Studies, 22*(3), 253-275.

Newmann, F. (1991). Higher order thinking in the teaching of social studies: Connections between theory and practice. In J. F. Voss, D. N. Perkins, & J. W. Segal (Eds.), *Informal reasoning and education.* Hillsdale, NJ: Lawrence Erlbaum Associates.

Ortega y Gasset, J. (1958). *Man and crisis.* New York: Norton.

Peck, M. S. (1978). *The road less traveled.* New York: Simon and Schuster.

Perkins, D. N. (1992). *Smart schools: From training memories to educating minds.* New York: Free Press.

Polkinghorne, D. (1988). *Narrative knowing and the human sciences.* Albany: State University of New York Press.

Postman, N. (1992). *Technopoly: The surrender of culture to technology*. New York: Knopf.

Pribram, K. (1985). Mind and brain, psychology and neurosciences, the eternal verities. In S. Koch & D. E. Leary (Eds.) *A century of psychology as science*. New York: McGraw Hill.

Purkey, W. & Novak, J. M. (1984). *Inviting school success: A self-concept approach to teaching and learning* (2nd ed.). Belmont, CA: Wadsworth Publishing.

Saul, J. R. (1992). *Voltaire's bastards: The dictatorship of reason in the West*. New York: Free Press.

Schrag, F. (1988). *Thinking in school and society*. New York: Routledge.

Senge, P. M. (1990). *The fifth discipline: The art and practice of the learning organization*. New York: Doubleday.

Sizer, T. R. (1992). *Horace's compromise: The dilemma of the American high school*. Boston: Houghton Mifflin.

Smith, F. (1986). *Insult to intelligence: The bureaucratic invasion of our classrooms*. Portsmouth, NH: Heinemann.

Smith, F. (1988). *Joining the literacy club: Further essays into education*. Portsmouth, NH: Heinemann.

Smith, F. (1990). *To think*. New York: Teachers College Press.

Smith, F. (1993, July). Speech given at the Third Conference on Thoughtful Teaching and Learning, Brigham Young University. Provo, UT.

Solway, D. (1989). *Education lost: Reflections on contemporary pedagogical practice*. Toronto, ON: OISE Press.

Solway, D. (1993, July). Lecture, Department of Educational Leadership, Brigham Young University, Provo, UT.

Taylor, C. (1989). *Sources of self*. Boston: Harvard University Press.

Tinder, G. E. (1980). *Community: Reflections on a tragic ideal*. Baton Rouge: Louisiana State University Press.

UASSP (Utah Association of Secondary School Principals Newsletter). (1995, March). UASSP outstanding secondary principal of the year, *VASSP Newsletter*, p. 1.

U.S. Department of Labor, Secretary's Commission on Achieving Necessary Skills. (1992). *Learning a living: A blueprint for high performance: A SCANS report for America 2000*. Washington, DC: Author.

Utah State Office of the Legislative Fiscal Analyst. (1992). *Utah state public education strategic plan 1992-1997: A strategic guide for the future development of the public school system.* Salt Lake City: Author.

Webb, C., Shute, R., & Grant, K. (1994). *Teaching "thoughtfully" is not an oxymoron.* Unpublished paper, Department of Educational Leadership, Brigham Young University, Provo, UT.

Wiggins, G. (1989, November). The futility of trying to teach everything of importance. *Educational Leadership, 47*(3), 44-48, 57-59.

About the Authors

Clark D. Webb is a professor in the Department of Educational Leadership at Brigham Young University. His academic interests include the relationships between belief and action in the lives of leaders, the influence of technocratic thinking on schooling, and the possibility of thoughtful learning by students— kindergarten through graduate school. His non-academic interests are his family and primitive camping and hiking.

Larry K. Shumway is principal at Mountain High School, an alternative school in the Davis School District in suburban Salt Lake City. He has previously written about school change and the leadership of change in schools. Other interests include his family, history, and the more-than-occasional round of golf.

R. Wayne Shute is a professor in the Department of Educational Leadership at Brigham Young University. His chief academic interest is educational leadership pertaining to teaching and learning. He has published many articles, chapters in books, etc., both in the United States and in foreign countries. Dr. Shute is a long distance runner. He and his wife, Lorna, are the parents of nine children, and they have nineteen grandchildren.